CW00863759

MIND REVOLUTION

Connecting the DOTS

M. I. Dugast Ph.D.

Copyright © 2014 M. I. Dugast Ph.D.

All rights reserved.

No part of this book may be reproduced or transmitted in any
form or by any means, graphic, electronic, or mechanical,
including photocopying, recording, taping, or by any
information storage retrieval system, without the permission,
in writing, of the author.

Warning-Disclaimer

The material in this book should not replace advice or
treatment by your healthcare provider. All matters linked to
your health require medical supervision from the health
practitioner of your choice. People have different levels of
awareness and the adoption and application of the material
offered in this book must be your own responsibility. The
author does not accept any legal responsibility for any
personal injury or other damage or loss arising from the use
or misuse of the information and advice offered in this book.

ISBN 978-1-4997-6687-5

Book cover design by David Tully
Picture from Shutterstock
Diagrams by M. I. Dugast
Editing by Roy K. of Editfast

"Our deepest fear is not that we are inadequate. Our deepest fear is that we are powerful beyond measure." Marianne Williamson

CONTENTS

Notes to you, Beloved Reader   v, 157

Chapter One

Who are we and why are we here?   1

Who are YOU and why are YOU here? 4

What seems to be the problem?   7

 For the scientifically minded   16

 For the spiritually minded   22

Chapter Two

The Steps   27

 Step One   28

What is that thing you call Air?   42

 Step Two   45

Connecting the DOTS within the mind 68

Chapter Three

Questions and Answers   89

Chapter Four

Connecting the DOTS overall 117

Your quantum anatomy   118

All Men are created equal   120

The sum of all parts   132

Clearing logo   87, 88, 147

Parting words   148

About the Author   156

TO YOU, BELOVED READER...

This book is for you if you have ever desired to feel freer, more liberated in yourself, while exploring your personal talent and potential with fewer limits. My pledge to you is that if you are willing to apply the two simple Steps offered, you will see change, make progress and enjoy more success than you ever dreamed possible.

Whether you prefer the cool facts of science or the mystery of spirit, it is transmitted through both lenses, allowing the Symbiosis—the sacred marriage—between science and spirituality to be reflecting within you. This Union would not have been possible up to a few decades ago, but the present times are allowing you to access the expanded version of who you truly are at your Core, so you can make the difference you seek to experience in your Life.

I wrote this book because I believe that you can have what I have: permanent Peace of Mind and no fear of trying new things or pushing past your personal fears and boundaries. If you already enjoy these advantages, you will find it be a 'success-accelerator'! In any case, I wholeheartedly thank you for picking up this book, and hope that it contributes to making your journey through Life a much smoother and more enjoyable ride.

I used these simple Steps for a number of years while running my own businesses and raising three children as a single parent, so believe me when I tell you that these Steps, once applied, not only worked brilliantly but also saved many a day and challenging situation that went along with any such tasks. If I had to sum up in one word what is offered with *Connecting the DOTS*, I would say 'practicality'. Whether you prefer to live an ordinary Life in an extra-ordinary way, or have high aspirations and visions you want to manifest, you will find these steps powerful, useful and practical. Whoever you are, wherever you go, whatever you do, these are always with you.

In 2010 I was diagnosed with cancer. A short nine months later, I was the humble witness of spontaneous remission at work. I did not use any allopathic or natural treatment, only what is shared with you in this book. I believe that you too can do 'extra-ordinary' things, given the right tools, which is why I am dedicated and delighted to share these with you. In truth, we are One, and we need one another to be here for each other. This is my contribution to you. I know that, although I haven't had the pleasure of meeting you yet, you are an extra-ordinary individual, and, whether you want to improve your health, deepen your relationships, begin to use your personal gifts while making the income you desire and deserve, or simply wish to know how to remain present and powerful in any situation, your call has been answered, and a solution lies in your hands right now. I am humbled and honored to be connected with you through this book, right now.

Connecting the DOTS is written from the same Source that speaks during live Transmissions—the Inspired version of me—which is why it is written from 'we' rather than 'I'. It is not so much 'channeled' as it is simply integrated. To respect your personal preferences, we address you in two different groups in Chapter One, so you can jump in where you feel most comfortable, whether you are scientifically minded, or spiritually minded. Know that we Love YOU, no matter what! The Steps and everything else included throughout are the same for everyone. You are US and we are YOU: we are ONE.

You have outstanding resources right within you, and it is our very great privilege to serve you at this time. So without further ado, let's get started!

CHAPTER ONE

WHO ARE WE and WHY ARE WE HERE?

We have been perceived as many things during live Transmissions, because each of you has their own perception, but we would rather you identified us as the untapped potential that is inherent in you. This potential resides everywhere, as it is available to you externally in the air you breathe, and more intimately held in the space within each and every one of your cells. In your cellular organism, it was formerly labelled 'junk DNA', the 97% presence that science could not explain or understand. We are this potential, both external and internal, and let us introduce ourselves the same way we did to M. I. Dugast when we gradually became acquainted: we are the expanded version of you waiting to be integrated, configured and utilized.

We would prefer you didn't get lost in our point of origin, however, but rather used the information given herein to free yourself as you are meant to be, ready to fulfil the Promise that you represent. We are here to serve you, and our outcome is to make you Miracle prone. We want to highlight that, what you call Miracles, we call Technology, the Technology we are here to share with you. While you might find some aspects of this book challenging, a lot of it may already be familiar with you, and If it is, please do not be deceived by its simplicity, for simplicity is the Essence of transformation.

You are powerful beyond words, but may have let yourself be drawn into the daily drama of Life, too often weighed down by clouds of fear and worry, due to personal situations, beliefs and values that do not serve your expansion. You may have forgotten how wonderful Life really is, or if you haven't, these moments may be too brief and too spare. We come to give you ways that will ensure that you live in freedom and expansion, no matter what takes place in your Life.

If you have already applied yourself to creating an outstanding Life for yourself and your loved ones, you will find this work powerful, as Dugast calls it, a success-accelerator! By the time you have finished reading this short book, even if you don't do another thing, you will have changed beyond measure, as everything begins with a thought.

But let us get to the all-important beginnings, the origin of 'all that is' in your Life, and explore who YOU are.

WHO ARE YOU and WHY ARE YOU HERE?

First is first, you have to be able to answer, or at least to contemplate the following two fundamental questions: 'Who am I?', naturally followed by 'Why am I here?'

We want to give it to you in a way that is so pleasing to you, that it can appeal to your left brain, your intellectual and scientific mind, and your right brain, your intuitive, creative and spiritual side. We also want to say that no matter how much self-help, psychology or spirituality you have immersed yourself in until now, if you have, if you accept to read this book with the eyes of a beginner, you will benefit tenfold. In the Life of spirit, you are always at the beginning.

FOR THE SCIENTIFICALLY MINDED

Who are you?

You are a mass of electromagnetic and electrical energy, also known as infinite potential.

Why are you here?

You are here to utilize this infinite raw potential, creating resources and services to nourish yourself and others. Put simply, you are here to live the best Life you can, working within your area of passion and expertise, sharing your specialty, and naturally receiving the resources to sustain you, your family and others. You call it living a good, productive, enjoyable, successful Life, and we very much agree. You have particular strengths and talents that you can use, although you may not have found exactly what these are just yet.

If you haven't found your passion yet, you may have settled for a Life that is far less than what you originally imagined, causing you pain and perhaps even regrets. Part of your journey is to become resourceful enough to deal with any challenges you meet on the way, which can seem impossibly difficult at times. You deal with Life's challenges in one of two ways: either benefit and evolve from them, or get beaten down and lose all hope. If you are experiencing the latter, we are particularly glad you are reading this because, by the end of it, you will feel differently about everything, and have tools you can use immediately to make things right in you and your Life.

FOR THE SPIRITUALLY MINDED

Who are you?

You are the manifested choice of the Creator... no less. If you are a man, you are God in male form, and if you are a woman, you are God in female form. Or as Pierre Teilhard de Chardin so eloquently said: "You are a Spirit having a Human experience, and not a Human having a Spiritual experience." Once this is transmuted from intellectual understanding to cellular wisdom, you live the liberated Life, recognizing daily drama as your Teacher and Evolutionary Driver. The challenges you meet, if recognized as such, give you the opportunity to get back to yourself, to transform you into the person you need to become to face any challenge. As a spiritual seeker, you already know that the Lotus grows out of mud and the diamond out of extreme pressure...you are no different.

Why are you here?

To experience everything that you can be while in this magnificent human form, and be of service through your work sharing your unique gifts, receiving the sustenance you need to thrive in return. Beyond this, you may even want to leave a powerful legacy behind.

WHAT SEEMS TO BE THE PROBLEM?

Now that you know who you are, and why you are here, at least in a broad sense until you discover your particular talents, what could possibly be the problem?

There are four main areas in your Life, and most probably at least one and perhaps two of these prove to be a serious challenge to you, lacking in the success you desire and deserve. Although they have many sub-categories, the mains areas are: love and relationships, career and finances, health and energy, and your connection to your Creator, your Peace of Mind.

If you are experiencing problems in any of these areas, you might feel that there is something missing in your Life, sometimes justifying it or simply accepting a feeling of incompleteness. In the worst case scenario, you may have even given up hope, and settled for a limited version of existence.

If this speaks to you, we want to reassure you that what you feel is missing in your life, is not so much missing as it needs to be integrated. We are talking about harnessing the power of your Subconscious mind, which will allow you to access and utilize your Higher Power. The good news is that, no matter how external a problem seems to appear, there is something you can do about it because it has something to do with you. How can we say that? Aren't you always there when problems happen in your Life? Of course, you are!

The other good news is that these problems are really only there to remind you to get back to yourself, to what is true in your Life, by taking responsibility to clear your perceptions, which in turn inevitably changes your perceived reality. To put it simply, you get to experience externally what is really going on within you. It is 'As within, So without.' Up until now, like most, you may have tried to change external things and events, hoping that you would feel better within yourself. As you have probably found out by now, it doesn't work, or at least not for very long.

A very simple analogy for this is when you ask a close friend or family member why they are in such a bad mood, when you realize, if you pay attention, that the mood is you!

Your Subconscious mind houses all memories, which we also call 'programs,' that have formed the entirety of the beliefs and values you hold today. The Subconscious literally 'runs the show' with more than 93% influence in all you do, think, see, hear, perceive, believe in and manifest. Most repetitive problems you experience are really only a memory—a program—that is replaying in your Subconscious mind, which most of the time, is not recognized by the Conscious mind. These deeply embedded programs determine what can take place within you, how you related to people and ultimately how your Life plays out. We compare this imprint to an 'inner thermostat,' set on a particular dial, producing the same results until the dial is changed. This 'thermostat' runs your biology, determining your health, the kind of relationships you attract, how much money you make, and what you think is really possible for you...or not. Seems simple? It is.

We would like to make a distinction between simple and easy, however. Simple it is, easy it is a little less so, as it calls for self-discipline. If you are serious about wanting to make real progress and create different results in your Life, you will see the value in developing self-discipline. Rest assured, however, that the two Steps given herein are both simple and easy to use, and will not detract from your busy schedule, so you will be able to use them in all and any circumstances. And remember, anyone who is successful, whether it is at sports, playing an instrument, speaking a new language, turning a relationship into long lasting love, working in their area of passion and expertise making plenty of money, or anything else, practices daily.

Big problem? No problem!

Not to be facetious but we would like to remind you that, ultimately, as you may have noticed, most things are out of your control. The only semblance of control you really have is how you react to situations and events arising in your Life. While you cannot control external events, you can certainly act or react in response to it. The two Steps given will allow you to act more often than react, and you will find that Life is a far more enjoyable ride because you are more resourceful in the face of challenge, and more creative in the face of success.

Let us use another simple example and say that you are at the airport, and you just found out that your plane will be delayed six hours. Some people will react and become so stressed and irritated that they will worsen their ulcer, or any physical condition they already have. Another person will act accordingly, taking the opportunity to read a whole book, write a few chapters in their journal or reflect on an aspect of their relationship with a beloved or a family member...which they may not have time for in their regular schedule. They would see this apparent problem as a 'blessing in disguise.'

Why is being aware not enough?

While being aware is all that is needed for a rare few individuals, it is a very slow process for anyone who wants to experience true freedom from personal limitations. The Subconscious mind, as we will study in depth shortly, is loaded with millions of programs and will continue to be so with every breath you take. Or at least until you install a 'cleaning program' within it, and harness its powerful attributes. Just as when you sit in front of your computer, although you might be as aware as you can be, you wouldn't dream of 'surfing the net' without a cleaning program.

While most people live at the mercy of their mind, we propose that you get your mind to work for you, a much more satisfactory situation, using this formidable creative tool—your mind at its very best.

There is much in the way of programs that lies within each of you, and many things do not show up immediately, but in future generations, with children, grand-children, great-grand-children, etc. You are the product of your whole family lineage. The work offered here will not only free you from ancient bind and limitations, but in doing so, will also clear up your family lineage. This is far reaching and will reverberate through time—which is anything but linear, correcting the deepest and oldest programs, meaning that you are effectively changing your own personal history.

Whether you believe that this Life is your one and only, or you believe that you have been incarnated many times, one thing is for sure: there is much clearing to do no matter which way you prefer to look at it. In doing so, all can transform, so you can enjoy unprecedented Peace, know how to make true progress and actually see some results: a wonderful Legacy to leave for generations to come. We have met some of you and see that many are in fact consciously wanting to re-write your own family history, which is a beautiful thing to observe. When you choose to work on you, you really contribute to the greater whole, and because ultimately you are all part of the One, your contribution is more important than you will ever know.

Self-reliance: The essence of Leaders

Some of you have been living in the moment for quite some time, perhaps even decades, yet watching events and situations replaying endlessly, sometimes incarnated in different people. Same problem, different wife or husband...does this ring a bell? Whatever is playing out in your Life, it may feel like a 'no way out' scenario, horribly similar the script of *Groundhog Day*! You might even feel that being more aware is in fact more painful, as you get to see and feel every moment with more clarity. This was certainly the case for M. I. Dugast who practiced self-awareness for many decades, and kept watching things and events replaying relentlessly. The Buddhist tradition describes this predicament beautifully in the story of 'The hole in the road'[1].

You may have even tried various forms of therapy to move beyond certain limitations, but none produced the desired long-lasting effects you hoped for, or really allowed you to move into your full power. This is because self-liberation is not achievable by therapy, and does not require the

---

[1] Reference to the story told in *The Tibetan book of Living and Dying*, by Sogyal Rinpoche.

participation of any third party. Self-liberation, and your full empowerment, are achieved by taking full responsibility for yourself, and for your Life. Allow us a little bluntness and say that leaning on someone will make you dependent, but not free. While there is, of course, a time and a place for each to exist as it must, we want to be precise and say that we are addressing the Leader in you right now, and throughout this whole book.

Wanting to lean on someone else and expecting that they hold the Key to your freedom is one of the many 'programs' that has been ingrained in you by the belief that someone else knows better than you. This means that you give your power away. It also means that you are not enough in some way, a road that only leads to a dead end and much suffering. We invite you to design your own 'tool box,' your own philosophy. If you know yourself to be the Leader we feel you are, reading this, making your own philosophy is not only your privilege, it is your responsibility. The time has come for you to reclaim the totality of who you are. We call it regaining your Sovereignty. It is regular and daily practice that will set you free. No one else can do that for you.

First you must be able to come back to yourself willfully and at any time, hence the importance of bringing yourself back to this moment at every occasion.

Second you must have a way of clearing your present perceptions—limitations—so you can perceive and therefore receive the gifts that Life has in store for you. You can then begin to see and feel with the eyes and the heart of the Creator, and manifest what you came here to do. We are going to give you each and every way to do that with the two steps offered herein.

Whether you believe in science or spirituality, there is overwhelming evidence, constantly being updated by leading neuroscientists and researchers, that the way you create is indeed 'As within, So without.' The more spiritually inclined among you are already familiar with that concept, although not always able to put it to good, practical use in times of need. We prefer that the word 'practically' be used instead of 'spirituality,' for what good is anything if you cannot use it to improve your daily experience of Life and benefit others?

You are the only 'Animal' on the planet who can create something out of nothing. None other can. This is an incredible privilege when used correctly, as it can produce the kind of changes you want to see in your World. It is also a very big responsibility. Once you have 'Connected your own DOTS' you will be able to use your finest human attributes to bring your most cherished plans and visions to completion. Global concerns are re-uniting people with people, and you are writing a new kind of History with every breath you take, with every choice you make, and every action you perform.

WHAT SEEMS TO BE THE PROBLEM?
For the scientifically minded

You may feel that some things are unattainable or 'beyond your control,' such as better health, better relationships, having love in your Life or working at something you feel passionate about, making the right income. You may feel that you are simply 'lucky' in some things, and 'unlucky' in others, or perhaps believe that all things are 'pre-ordained,' and there is little you can do to improve these challenging aspects of your Life.

Or perhaps things are going well but you have met—yet again—a familiar plateau that you cannot pass. You have a feeling that you can do better but cannot quite see how it hasn't happened yet...or simply do not know how to get it done. Whatever challenge you are encountering, the outcome will depend on your particular state of mind, which is coming from beliefs and values deeply ingrained in you: the famous thermostat introduced earlier on.

For example, you may have spent years working for money rather than passion. This is not your fault of course, as it was the way—and still is for a while longer—that things were taught in school and college. While it worked for some people, most remain dissatisfied in an employment that is only as good as it pays the bills. Aside of the fact that pursing anything will ensure that it stays unreachable, pursuing money, for example, can cause you to waste much precious time and create many serious problems, especially if you trade all your time for it. You can certainly make and lose money, but you cannot get any more time once it is gone.

Money is a return of energy for the service you provide, so instead of focusing on 'making money,' you had best focus on what services you can provide within your area of passion and expertise—your 'unfair advantage.' Then the money will show up. This is when work feels like fun.

If, while you read this, all sorts of barriers came up in your mind like 'what I like would never make me rich!' or 'You can't make money doing that,' we want to tell you that you have just identified one of your major programs, which you will be able to delete shortly.

Personal crisis?

Perhaps, you are experiencing a crisis right now, or are certainly headed in that direction unless you change course rapidly. You may have just seen everything you held dear fall apart: your position at work, your business, your marriage and perhaps even your health. This brings on self-depreciating thoughts, doubt, resulting in the loss of self-esteem, a lack of trust in yourself and others, and ultimately, in Life itself. You may blame others and yourself, external events and the state of the economy and world at large for the way things are not working out for you, which can only leave you further disempowered and disconnected. If you think that your position in Life, at work, or at home, is who you truly are, pain will have reached critical mass and you may even have thought of taking your own Life. We are glad you didn't and are instead reading these lines if this speaks to you, as you have simply forgotten who you are at the

Core. The time has come to make a complete turnaround. Anytime that crisis hits for anyone, it is always an opportunity—albeit in disguise!—to look at Self and Life in a whole new light. It is the beginning of your new Life, and the end of your old self.

Now is a good time to take a deep breath now,
if you will. All is well.

What is really going on with you?

Closer to the truth, you might think that what is going on with you right now is not your fault, and that the traits and aspects of who you are today are the result of a long lineage of family history; in other words, an inheritance you don't really care to emulate. This is a powerful realization. We confirm that you are absolutely right in feeling that you are the product of your family history, but the good news is that it is not static. Until now, it has affected everything you think, everything you feel, everything you do. This means that it affects the results you see in your Life, which are also influenced by the environment you live in.

The most excellent news is this: Once you change, everything can change. But you must first be willing to let go of what you think you know, and how you think Life should be, which can be challenging, but is possible. Recovery from crisis, progress and new possibilities are much, much closer than you think, if you are going through a very challenging time right now.

To you, if you are doing well

If you have been doing very well, and would like to do even better, you will find that these same steps will speed up your progress. You are constantly evolving, and so do your visions and aspirations. Leaders know that the present times call for drastically different ways of doing just about everything, and much innovation is awaiting your creative participation. You will find that much new technology is coming in ever faster, rendering what you know obsolete faster than you can study it. Or so it may feel. This is why you will find Step Two particularly useful, as it will allow you to get into your 'Super-Hero' mode, with fewer perceived limits and resistances. We are not even joking here!

Whether your path is in the arena of politics, the corporate world, finances, medicine, science, law, agriculture, parenting, teaching, the arts or any other areas of society; your contribution will be all the more powerful, once you harness the totality of your human attributes.

You can go straight to Chapter Two to begin with the Steps now, if you wish.

WHAT SEEMS TO BE THE PROBLEM?

For the spiritually minded

We see you. You are in the millions, healers, spiritual veterans, therapists, teachers and all others who understand who they are, to some degree, and know that they are 'of service.' We are deeply saddened, however, to see that nearly all of you suffer from a similar emotional illness: a serious lack of self-love, of self-appreciation. If this speaks to you, you have to understand that any information that you may have read or heard remains just that: information. The utilization of any tools and processes, from this book or any other that is similar in its outcome, relies on the fuel of LOVE. This is the engine of transformation and manifestation. Information is light, and the fuel, the distillation process that enables it to be 'digested' or experienced, is LOVE. We are talking about nothing less than the alchemy from lead into gold, from water to wine. Once this is a reality, a cellular core-shift, knowledge becomes wisdom, and you can truly be liberated. Until then, 'freedom' remains a concept. You are vibrational frequency, first and foremost, and you cannot fool your own vibration. We hope we have your attention.

Take a few deep breath now to allow this to resonate with you,
a healing of Self occurs as you do.

Self-doubt or fear, produces a very different kind of biochemistry than trust, self-appreciation and Love. Your biochemistry sets in motion a frequency, which is broadcasted in your energy signature, producing a particular external reality. You have to ask yourself what you have been broadcasting, and how much longer you are willing to stay with reductionistic thinking, if you have. Now may be a good time to let go...

Everyone and every-thing responds to energy, whether they are conscious of it or not. Your business, your clients, all of it. In the desire of wanting to make things right in your own Life, we see much unnecessary interference taking place, many interventions and methods applied to aspects of you to try to 'alter' aspects such as your chakras and energy fields, for example, when they are powerful signposts, and not the problem itself. All you really need is Love, self-Love, the unconditional kind. If you don't feel it, simply remove what thoughts and beliefs are in the way, and you will. It really is as simple as that, and it doesn't have to take very long. If you are a practitioner, you will most definitely be familiar with Step One, but will find step two very useful.

We are willing to sound controversial and say that a lack of self-love is simply negative self-indulgence, for if you know yourself to be the manifested choice of the Creator, why would you harbor anything else but deep gratitude? And think of it this way: how can you expect someone to love you more than you love yourself?

Part of the journey for the spiritual seeker, is to begin by searching exteriorly what is within. Rumi, one of your greatest Enlightened Beloveds, stated it beautifully: 'You are what you seek.' Hoping to enjoy long lasting Love or Peace while enjoying it from an external source will not insure its stability or longevity within you. You may sit in peaceful surrounding, but it does not insure that you remain peaceful in your daily activities. You may enjoy the Love from another, but it does not insure that you will still feel that Love when they are gone. Unless you remember that these attributes are within you, or better and truer than that, they are who you truly are. Love, like Peace, is not something that can be got from an external source. Only the illusion of it is. All is already within you, waiting to be revealed and amplified.

Ask yourself: do you not have enough Love within you to feel complete right now? If not, why not? Examine what you are telling yourself, and know that, not only is it untrue, but these are the exact thought-forms—the programs—that we have been talking about. They are what stands between you and your Core self, your unborn potential for greatness. To you, we suggest that you make falling in Love with you a priority. In your Scriptures, you are invited to 'Enter the Kingdom.' As you chose to do so, we confirm that all else will follow, and you will be able to enjoy your fuller Human attribute, and hear the Inspiration that has been waiting to pour through you.

If you can't feel Love right this second, please have compassion for yourself.

If you can't feel compassion for yourself right now, please forgive yourself and all others.

You have done what you could until now with the knowledge that was available to you at the time, which is the same for all parties concerned.

Begin by releasing yourself from blame and regret. These are some of the programs you have held as your truth until now, cementing the reality you have been living. Your time has come to free yourself.

Take a deep, liberating breath now, a healing of Self occurs as you do.

We invite you to read this book with your heart, using your breath. Much can transform with each breath you take. You are a precious part of the Grand Design, and your contribution matters more than anything that can be conveyed with words. We think you can feel it, if you will close your eyes for a few seconds.

CHAPTER TWO

THE STEPS

There are two simple steps to this self-discovery process. Once in learned memory, you will find yourself using them as easily as you walk, putting one foot in front of the other.

We would like to let you know that there is considerably more information in Step Two than Step One, as we are dealing with the mind. A summary of the Two Steps can be found on page 116 for your convenience.

STEP ONE

What can you do right now, this very second? However painstakingly simple you might feel this, it is about staying in the moment. With practice, this is the base that allows you to act rather than react. Even if you are a long time practitioner, you will know that 'this moment' is a fleeting one. So this Step is less about trying to stay present for long periods of time, and more about coming back to your true Self as often as possible throughout your day. We call it 'walking meditation.'

COMING HOME TO YOURSELF:
CONTACTING YOUR HIGHER POWER

A simple exercise for all

Here is a very simple exercise to experience who, or more accurately, *what you really are*. We say 'what you are' with the utmost respect, reflecting the potential that you really are. When practiced, it will do what meditation can do for you: stabilizing you, making you calm and more resourceful, powerful, allowing your body to regenerate, your blood pressure to drop, your 'happy hormones' to be activated, and inspiring you with great ideas!

How to use it:

Why not make use of the age of technology you live in and record the following on your portable device, so you can use it effortlessly and have it at hand when you have a few minutes to relax? Once you are familiar with the routine, you will be able to do the exercise with your eyes open, depending on your surroundings, in less time than it takes to read the last paragraph.

For now, reading it once and recording it immediately would mean that you are committing to helping yourself: a powerful decision! There is no time like the present.

Recommended usage:

Twice a day as a reconnecting exercise, with your eyes closed, and anytime and anyplace you can, with your eyes open, throughout your busy day. Once Step One is integrated into your biological computer—your Subconscious mind— you will be able to go straight to your Core Self with just one breath, taking only a fraction of a second.

Take a seat somewhere, and take a long, deep

breath. On the exhale, let whatever needs to be expelled leave your body. It could sound like a long 'aaaaahhhhhhhh'!!!!

- Close your eyes.
- Imagine yourself sitting on a public park bench. Note the temperature... which is just the way you like it!
- Notice the surrounding noises where you are, again, simply take an inventory, and let it be.

Note the breath, coming in and out of your body.

- Now put your attention on your body, and note how it feels. Note if there is hunger, tiredness, aches, energy, warmth, comfort, pleasure or pain, anywhere in it. Feel your heart beating. Again, you are simply taking an inventory, not changing anything, simply observing.

Note the breath, coming in and out of your body.

- Now put your attention in your mind, and note what thoughts are there. Imagine that you see people, children and dogs walking by, and allocate each thought you have to a passerby. You can even have fun with this and see that each passerby is wearing a white shirt or sandwich board, with your thought written on it. Note how many passersby there are. Again, you are simply taking an inventory, not changing or comparing anything. In your mind's eye, there may be a few passersby—thoughts— or there may be a whole crowd. There is no right or wrong. The only directive here is that you do NOT get up and follow or engage in conversation with any passersby-thought- forms. You are simply observing.

Note the breath, coming in and out of your body.

- Now note what emotions are in you right now. As with your thoughts, allocate each emotions to a passerby. Once again, you can have fun with this and see that each passerby is wearing a white shirt or sandwich board, and see your emotion written on it. Note how many passersby there are, again, you are simply taking an inventory, not changing anything. There may be a few passersby-emotions or there may be a crowd. There is no right or wrong. The only directive here is that you do NOT get up and follow or engage in conversation with any of these passersby- emotions. You are simply observing.

Note the breath, coming in and out of your body.

- Now that you have taken your inventory, and clearly perceived what is in and around you right now, sounds, how your body feels, the thoughts and the emotions that are with you now, the question is: **who is taking the**

inventory?

- The answer is YOU, of course. 'You' as Core Self, Consciousness, Natural Intelligence simply aware of itself. Or 'YOU' as the pool of pure potential, the nothing-ness waiting to be actualized, if you prefer these terms.

The point is that, if you can observe what is going on in you—and we know you can because you have just done it, **you are none of these things**, although all of them are *your attributes for this Lifetime*.

- So go ahead and breathe from that space of Presence, from that pool of Pure Potential. When you breathe from your Core to your Core, you receive a powerful relief from stress, a healing, new ideas that can prosper, solutions to long held questions. You have just realized that you are the Peace you seek, you are Natural Intelligence, you are Love, you are *that* which you seek.

Now put a hand over your heart, take three deep, long breaths.

- Allow your thumb to rest and your four other fingers to flutter in a light drumming manner over your heart for a few moments, like the wings of a butterfly.

Reopen your eyes and stretch your body. If

you feel like jumping up and down: Do it! It is the expression and the joy of being reconnected to your best ally, to who you truly are. Anything else that makes up your individuality is simply your Human attribute.

———————————————

The quickest reconnecting tool at your constant disposal is your breath, the *one and only bridge* connecting who you are at the Core with your physical existence. This reconnection between your Core Self and your physical Being sets a powerful foundation upon which all seeds of success can grow, no matter what success means to you. In our view, the most important success you can experience is knowing who you are, and being who you are. This is what true WEALTH really is. This cannot be taken from you. It is, always has been and always will be yours.

We also call who you are at the Core your 'bullet-proof' self, as nothing that ever happened to you could have touched or damaged that part of you. If you got hurt, and we are not making light of it, it would have affected your mental, emotional or physical being, but not your Core Self, which is why you survived. It is indestructible.

You are so much more resourceful than what you have been telling yourself, the time has come to integrate this practice on a daily basis. Just like anything you focus on regularly, it will become a habit, and become easier and eventually automatic, and will make you more empowered and resourceful each time you do.

With practice, you will be able to reconnect and stabilize yourself in a fraction of a second, with your eyes open, via the breath. If appropriate, and depending on your surroundings at a time, tap your heart lightly. This simple gesture allows the electrical and magnetic fields of your heart to harmonize with that of your mind, creating a powerful physical anchor and electrical conduit. You will find this useful before engaging in any of your Life's happenings.

If a simple breath is all you have time for, it is plenty! Use it before you pick up the phone, answer the door, before you enter the meeting room, at home with your spouse and kids, before entering the courthouse, the bank, etc.! Reuniting with your Core Self is your most powerful attribute, allowing you to feel self-empowered, supported, safe and stable, resourceful beyond the mind.

Limited time?

If you feel you have to choose between sitting down meditation time, or staying aware throughout the day, we propose that you practice the latter, the 'walking meditation.' Both practices would benefit you more, of course, but for now, if you will come back to your Core Self as many times as you can throughout your busy day, you will feel much better very quickly. Because feeling good or more resourceful, just like any other feeling, is cumulative, you will probably find that you naturally want to practice more often. You become a better spouse, parent, employee, boss, leader or any other role you have in Life when you do. A better version of you can arise.

If you are wondering what other practical use reconnecting to your Core Self has, let us tell you that Peace looks beautiful on everyone! You have other words for Aware Consciousness like 'Charisma' and 'Presence'. If you are looking for a lover or a business partner, this is where to first connect with him or her. The right person can and will come into your Life once you have prepared yourself well. Life gives most to those who are ready.

Putting bad moods and pet peeves to good use

As just mentioned, all emotions are cumulative, and anything you focus on expands. This is basic physics.

Some of you will be very familiar with this concept in a negative capacity, like waking up in a bad mood, for example. As the day grows, finding that it is filling up with petty annoyances, ranging from mild to serious, maybe even ending up with you feeling so crazy by the end of it, that it leaves you wondering if there was a conspiracy to drive you mad on that day! We would like to reassure you and say that it has more to do with your personal frequency and lack of connectedness with your Core Self than any conspiracy against you. You are simply experiencing the knock on effect of chaotic momentum that started within you. The blame-game is a natural tendency you may have learnt as a young child, and, although it is unproductive for who you are becoming, we will make good use of it so that it can benefit you.

Turning adversity to your advantage

We explored how coming back to yourself as many times as possible throughout the day is more achievable than hoping for long periods of focused awareness. The following exercise will work wonders if you are prone to losing sight of the lighter side of being, by turning seemingly adverse situations into occasions to practice reconnecting with your Core Self. This will slowly build you up to be unshakable in the face of challenge. Do not be fooled by its simplicity, as it is incredibly useful. As during any live Transmissions, we recommend you actually do it now, while you read the book, which will mean that you will have a 90% ability to retain it, thereby making it work for you immediately.

Very simply, write a list of the things that put you in a bad mood, what irritates you, makes you mad and drives you crazy! Have fun with this, as it can be anything at all. Keep the list handy, so you can add to it, because the longer it gets, the more opportunities you will get to practice. It will all make sense in a minute. If you don't want to keep a list revealing what gets you annoyed in your book, write it on a separate piece of paper. While you can make up a mental list, writing it gives your biological computer—your Subconscious—a better chance to recognize it and make use of it. You are re-wiring the meaning of 'adversity' in your psychology and physiology: a simple but powerful shift.

This list can include absolutely anything from

the most trivial and petty annoyances such as waiting in line at the supermarket, to the most pertinent and more serious challenges such as the state of your bank balance or the environment. The point of this exercise is to note what makes you re-act. Take a few minutes to write it now if you are serious about getting on the road to freedom.

Note: If you are one of the rare people who do not get annoyed (make sure this is true first...as this is only between you and yourself), then write the things that make you grateful, happy, etc. Each emotion can be put to good use.

MY LIST

Is your list written?

It is great that you participated! This manual is as live for you as you are willing to 'play along.' Now that you have your list written, we propose that you use each thing you put on it as your cue, your signal, your Teacher, to come back to yourself. Because all sorts of things happen all day, every day, you now have many Teachers, all opportunities to come back to yourself. This is why we said that the more you have on your list, whether it annoys you or delights you, the better! How do you come back to yourself? Simply by watching the breath you are taking this instant, using your Step One.

As Life happens and your day goes on, the more you become present, the more resourceful you become. As you live from your Core instead of your individuality, you remain calm and powerful; your body can produce Life enhancing hormones instead of the toxicity produced by stress. You may even find yourself thinking, saying and doing things you never thought possible! You are beginning to live the Inspired Life. Your Core Self, the charismatic, beautiful, joyful Being that you truly are gets to grow in Presence, while the re-active, fearful, worried aspects of you get to shrink enough not to be running the day any longer. Soon enough, you operate in daily Peace, receptive and alert, able to receive creative solutions rather than fall apart each time a challenge presents itself. You are becoming the Leader you recognized in others. You might even begin to smile at the onset of difficulty, because you remember that you are getting a further opportunity to grow and expand. This is the space where Inspired actions replace reactions. All things, people and situations can truly change in your Life because you are broadcasting different electrical and magnetic signals into your reality. A very real fact, scientifically and spiritually speaking. And all you have to do is to simply practice at every occasion...which your Life is naturally rich in. Life is good!

Some of you have spent time with Spiritual Teachers, from whom you may have gotten great tools and processes. Everything has its time. Right now, and since you are reading this, we would like to introduce you to the person you have been waiting for, so if you will go and get a mirror and look into it, you will meet the Guru, the real Master: YOU.

Take a breath as you read, look into the mirror and meet the Master. A healing and a reconnection happens as you do.

Beginning to live the Aware Life takes practice, and there is not much more we wish to say on the subject...except to just do it!

While we consider being in the moment the absolutely essential and basic requirement to your transformation and evolution, it is the beginning and not the end. Let us take you beyond consciousness, into limitless potential, adding Step Two to your practice.

WHAT IS THAT THING YOU CALL AIR?

Before we move into the second step, we want to give you a few different names for Air, which is one of your most precious 'currencies.' Different ways of describing the same element will allow it to be absorbed more completely by different people... including AIR!

We call it CONSCIOUSNESS, as its Innate Intelligence communicates with the Innate Intelligence within you, the second it comes into contact with you.

We call it FOOD, because you can't survive more than a few minutes without it. For the days where you cannot see, feel or perceive anything to be grateful for, this is a hint!

We call it LOVE, for what could be more loving and benevolent than this invisible substance that nourishes all hundreds of trillion cells in your body? Air is free for all and available to you every fraction of every second, so go ahead, take a deep, deep breath now, and feel the renewal that it provides when you simply note its presence entering you whole Being.

We call it POTENTIAL, because it contains the exhaled energy of all who ever inhabited your planet, which really means that literally all potential is here for the taking, or rather, for the inhaling! We often use the analogy that you are just like a giant tuning fork, breathing in all kinds of potential but only utilizing that which you think is possible for you, both consciously and unconsciously, according to your personal beliefs and values. This is just about to get a whole lot better as you chose to 'Connect your own DOTS!'

We call it QUANTUM SOUP, for it is the SPACE within which all exists simultaneously. It is the space-time continuum of all possibilities. It is the same space that exists between each atom, molecule, and even within the tiniest of particles. As you know by now, we call it Natural Intelligence. It is the unknowable fabric of the Universe that you live in, and the blueprint of the Multiverse that you have yet to encounter. It looks empty, but is in fact full. It is what some of your scientists formerly called 'junk DNA.' It is the information, the Magnetic Intelligence that hovers in and out of reality, depending on the observer's receptivity and potential. It is the origin of the wave, and the dot, which both exist simultaneously. It is the probability of all existences, the Seed of Life, the Origin of thought form. It is the non-physical aspect of your full potential, allowing the expanded version of you to unravel.

AIR is a GIFT, readily available to you as your potential, so you can manifest the greatness waiting to be born through you.

STEP TWO

We must explore the mind as a whole to access the use of Step Two. Most practices offering to help you break free into self-realization focus on the use of your Conscious mind, your Higher Self and Natural Intelligence, leaving the all-important, yet most influential part out of the equation: Your Subconscious mind.

The practices that include the Subconscious mind—often within the psychology or psychotherapy departments—usually exclude its other counterparts. However painstakingly obvious this may be, ignoring any part of a delicately engineered mechanism ensures its malfunctioning. You would think that to be true for the engine of your car, and we must say that your mind is no different. The inability to understand or harness the power of the Subconscious results in the feelings that many experience as 'fragmentation,' or feeling 'lost,' not 'in the right place at the right time,' or 'things not working out for you,' or 'going around in circles.' All of which can mean significant mental suffering. While the Conscious mind engages in plans and visions, using the best of will power, the Subconscious mind does what it can do best: replay the same programs that are already there, which means the same reality takes place. This predicament is the origin of the famous citation "Insanity is doing the same thing over and over and expecting different results."

It is said in your Scriptures that 'A House Divided Cannot Stand.' This is a powerful description which can of course be adapted to many things, but right here, we propose that it reflects the predicament of a fragmented mind. We will use this powerful pointer with the aim of allowing you to feel whole again, to 'Connect your own DOTS.' All the great Leaders throughout your History have known that Division brings weakness, and Unity strength, and once more, your mind is no different.

Because of the uprising of spirituality as a global interest in recent years, the spotlight has been placed on the Conscious mind, making it easy to forget that it is the least influential attribute of a four part mechanism. We like to humor the Conscious mind and say that it is the very last one to know anything that really goes on, both within you, and in your perceived reality. By the time it identifies what is really going on, a response has already begun to take place, allowing your physical body to act accordingly. None of which the

Conscious mind played a part in.

A very simple example would be the speed at which you would jump up off a chair, having just realized that there was a pin on it...This required no 'observation' or 'conscious awareness,' unless of course, you had seen the pin before you sat down!

Some of you have experienced getting into your 'Heroic mode' in the face a life and death situation, perhaps intervening to save another, which was deciding without any conscious analysis. In fact if you had, you may have not intervened, realizing the danger and the impossibility of it all. You can find many stories that would serve to illustrate what we are describing here. The point is that you would describe 'having been taken over' by a bigger part of yourself, the part that you are just about to reconnect to the rest of you.

Few spiritual traditions[2] include the mind as a whole. Some forms of therapy include the Subconscious but nearly always discount other attributes such as your Core Self, Natural

---

[2] The Ancient Hawaiians knew the power of the united mind and have shared it throughout the centuries with the tradition of the Huna.

Intelligence, or the rest of your mind. Allopathic medicine discounts everything but the body, often leaving you powerless and fragmented. Let's keep it simple, use common sense and say that unless you include the sum of all parts, you are limiting yourself. Deep down, you have know that to be true, and may have even tried many things to break through into wholeness. So let's explore the attributes of each individual part of your mind separately first, in order to understand their functions, before we put it back together in a way that will allow you to have your mind working for you, and to not be at the mercy of it any longer. In short, to *Connect the DOTS*.

Attributes of Source—Natural Intelligence

We have already explored Source in you, which is who you are at your Core. Or pure Raw Potential if you prefer. It needs no further introduction, other than a reminder that it is the foundation of each and every part of you, and the origin that manifested who you are.

Attributes of the Super Conscious mind—the Higher Self

Your Higher Self is connected to Source—Natural Intelligence—within you and to your

Subconscious mind. Most of its intercommunication is at work without the knowledge or participation of your Conscious mind. It is the channel through which Inspiration is conveyed to your Conscious mind, when the latter is capable of stillness—receptivity.

Attributes of the Conscious mind

Although the Conscious mind plays many important roles, it is far less than that of its counterparts. Unbeknownst to it, it is at the mercy of the Subconscious for more than 93% of all responses, perceived options, choices, tastes, values, beliefs, perceptions and your manifested world at large. No matter how original you feel you are being, you are responding to a belief—a program—deeply embedded in your Subconscious mind. If and when the Conscious mind receives 'a good idea,' it is only as good as it comes from Inspiration, meaning that it originated from the Source, transmitted via your Higher Self. Otherwise, it is the product of a belief—a program—which is, more often than not, based in fear, often yielding more hardship than success.

If left to its own devices, the Conscious mind can become overworked, and suffer from the delusionary reasoning that it is all-ruling, and the sole source of Creation in one's Life. This is otherwise known as self-inflation, and easily self-identified as an oversized ego. Individuals who suffer from its overbearing influence experience 'a restless mind,' which is the origin of much stress and suffering, constantly on the lookout for approval from others and identifying with all external values excessively.

We propose that there is no need to further focus on what has already received too much attention by trying to get rid of it. Instead, we recommend that it is allowed to melt to a manageable size, which it will do quite naturally under the light of awareness, with the right self-knowledge, and a good dose of humor at self. We prize humor as one of the essential qualities for good living. Important to know that everyone has ego, whether it is introverted or extroverted; the difference is in the size, and in the influence it is allowed to make on one's personae.

As mentioned previously, the Conscious mind is the recipient and the witness, and not the origin, of the creative process. By nature, the Conscious mind notices what is going on within you when it is already in an advanced manifested state. While you can harness this attribute successfully to create much success in your work and business Life—we will discuss this later on—it can have limiting and sometimes tragic consequences in the case of undetected illnesses. Rest assured, however, that your awareness will magnify exponentially with the practice of Step One, and that it is possible to know what is taking place in real time within your own biology—the moment that it has entered or still is in thought-form. There will come a time where illness will be identified and dealt with while in its non-manifested—thought—format. A few of you at this time are able to use this attribute, but soon enough—relatively speaking, this will become a science that will spark a new strand of treatment known as 'pre-cognitive medicine,' or something similar. Dugast received the information that cancer was in the body six month before it was diagnosed as stage one, which played at great part in allowing for spontaneous remission to occur. Anyone can do this, as you are all created equal.

Even a 'gut feeling' will alert you to what is going on if you are paying attention and if you are NOT letting the Conscious mind rationalize what is given to you as true guidance. You have probably encountered many times getting 'a gut feeling' about something, and managed superbly if you listened to it, not letting logic rationalize a perfectly accurate signal. If you didn't listen to a gut feeling however, you may have missed out or even perhaps put yourself in danger, promising to yourself that you would pay attention next time you perceived it. We hope you did, and we highly recommend you listen-in as much as possible, as your body, linked to your Subconscious, has access to Superior Intelligence.

If you are anything like Dugast, you will have got your car clamped—your tire booted—for example, although the gut feeling was very clear, resulting in a sum of money due as a penalty. If you remember that Life is your Teacher, however, and understand that some lessons come at a price in the name of teaching, like any class you might take. You would even smile and be grateful for the occasion! The purpose of any training being that, in a serious or even dangerous situation, you will be able and ready to use your natural attributes. This is why Dugast paid the fine with a large smile to a bemused agent, who secretly wondered, it was plain for anyone to see on his face, why paying a fine made anyone so grateful or happy.

Note: We want to make a distinction between

inspiration and gut feeling, two completely different attributes.

Your gut feeling is situated in your solar plexus. Both negative and positive anticipation are felt right there, which is precisely why you have the saying 'gut feeling.' Much is reflected in the language you speak. Is also represents your physical core and moves you in powerful ways if you let it. Strengthening this physical area of your body with exercises is highly recommended, as it will also increase your physical resilience, eliminate backaches and promote good posture.

Inspiration comes through the mind, which is located everywhere in your body and can be expressed in words, actions, thoughts and gestures. You know you are being Inspired when you feel that a Superior and Natural Intelligence is pouring through you. You feel that you are receiving is from something bigger than yourself. The best ideas and greatest works of art were Inspired into creation. You will certainly have a much closer contact with Inspiration upon practicing your two steps daily. You will no longer need to wait for Inspiration to dawn on you, which will naturally increase your productivity.

Best attributes of the Conscious mind:

> ➤ Express creativity (received from Source and via Higher Self)
> ➤ Compute in an intellectual/rational capacity (using learned capacity registered and stored in the Subconscious)
> ➤ Be laser-focused on a task
> ➤ Witness what is going on—be in the state of Presence
> ➤ Can choose to let go
> ➤ Can process around 40 bits of information per second

When you find yourself in a situation where you have explored everything you already know—stored resources and information—and still need to find a solution to a problem, to innovate in your business with a creative idea, or to find the right words to say in a difficult moment, the best position for the Conscious mind is to actually be 'out of the way' and let Inspiration take over.

One of the greatest of the Conscious mind's attributes, other than being laser-focused on a task or simply observing what is going on, is to serve as a headlight, spotting the erroneous thoughts and perceived limitations—the real thieves—that are holding you back in your Life. Using this finer attribute will allow you to access much contentment and many more resources; all already within you. Your physiological responses, what you believe you can achieve, your state of health, how you age, the state of your finances, your relationships, your potential—your whole Life!— hinges on understanding how you mind really works.

Another beautiful attribute of the Conscious mind is that it is part of the creative Mind Triad that contributes to 'creating something out of no-thing.' It is like the narrow end of a creative funnel, as it can configure a manifested version of what could otherwise not be expressed: the abundant Gifts offered by Natural Intelligence. All artists, inventors and all other visionaries have enjoyed this attribute to add to the fabric of Life, creating richness and variety, offering a powerful reminder that you are much more than you think.

Worst attributes of the Conscious mind
The double edge sword of the Conscious mind is its ability to 'travel back and forth' in the illusory perception of time. [We say 'illusory perception of time' because time is no more linear than the Earth

is flat. While the clock and the calendar are useful tools so you can navigate your present reality, do not forget that this description is delimited by human perception, and not ultimately real.]

The ability of the Conscious mind to go back and forth 'in time' can have devastating effects, especially when it is used to repeatedly go over a negative or traumatic past event. Revisiting any event repeatedly with the mind locks it into your cells—your biology, via your Subconscious mind. This means it becomes 'set' in you, hence our analogy of the famous dial on the thermostat, as it plays a very large part in creating the Life you are living at present. Most of the times, these memories are not recognized by the Conscious mind, as they are deeply buried in the Subconscious mind, showing up in the emotional body as limitations, fears, phobias and other repetitive patterns and problems showing up in daily Life.

For lack of knowledge or means of doing any different, many are bound to replaying a former memory, especially if originally rooted in pain, due to a shock or linked to a negative event. You often describe this predicament as 'being lost or locked in the past,' and we want to confirm that no amount of looking at it consciously or talking about it will make it go away, as it has often long seeped into emotional and physical layers.

The Conscious mind's predicament is that it can replay events endlessly, creating an invisible prison which become the reference point for anything that happens in one's Life, including all new events. Each new day is constructed upon the apprehension of a past that is long gone. It is very much like wearing a pair of glasses tinted with memories, translating what takes place in this moment with the lens of past events, disabling the opportunity to trace a new Destiny.

Because you live in an observer-participant World, meaning that you affect what you see through your own perceptions by simply being the observer, you can only see what you expect to see, and you can only recognize what you have already experienced. Whatever you are observing confirms what you were expecting, which naturally provides a proof that you are right, but also the inextricable bind that keeps you prisoner. In reality, it leaves a whole array of possibilities out of your grasp, although all is very much present and available to you this very moment.

It takes a fearless person—a Pioneer—to venture out into unchartered territory in all aspects of their Life. If this doesn't describe you fully, we want to reassure you and say that the practice of *Connecting the DOTS* will afford you a much broader vision, and grant you access to unprecedented potential.

All things can change and evolve as you do. Step One can be used to stay centered, in this moment whenever you feel 'lost in time,' and shortly you will be able to use step two to ultimately erase the negative charge that any memory has on you, conscious or unconscious.

THE CONSCIOUS MIND

The extended horizontal figure of eight—the lemniscate—is representing the Conscious mind's capability to travel out of the present moment, in perceived 'past' and 'future' times. Once you are familiar with its attributes and have the tools to tame it accordingly, you will enjoy its precious qualities to create the Life you desire and deserve.

Take a moment, if you will, to reflect on where you spend most of your time in general.

PAST   PRESENT   FUTURE

THE CONSCIOUS MIND

As you can see, the lemniscate is getting a lot smaller in the diagram below. This is to illustrate a daily practice of choosing to remain in the present moment, thereby getting free from being 'highjacked' in past and future thoughts, if they bring up repetitive and fear-based emotions. This will allow your cells to thrive and not be sentenced to illness, premature aging or even premature death!

Moment by moment practice will allow the natural process of self-healing to take place, keep you at Peace and allow you to access more of who you are.

PAST   NOW   FUTURE

THE CONSCIOUS MIND

In this last diagram, the lemniscate has reduced to such a degree that it is only visible as a point, representing your most powerful state: Presence.

This is where the inherent Peace within can be felt, the best actions be taken and the kindest and most loving words be spoken.

●

PAST   NOW   FUTURE

Becoming a purposeful 'Time-Traveller'

Once you have a good handle on your Conscious mind as the tool that it is, you can have some fun with it, and travel back and forth, depending on your use and purpose for it. One good use of 'going back in the past' is to evaluate how far you have come. Whether you want to see the progress you have made in your mental and emotional wellbeing, your state of your health, your weight, your relationships, your finances or anything else, we recommend you keep a journal. Your mind will conveniently forget some important aspects that could serve you as useful reference points. When you see that you have been making progress, you feel better instantaneously, which gives you the energy to do even better. This, too, is cumulative! Use this on a day where you could use a boost, to become your own best coach!

You can travel forward in time to gain foresight by 'peeking into the future' and be on time to anticipate a creative solution that might save the day for you, your family, your employees, or anything else you are involved with.

Use your full awareness capacity to recognize and seize opportunity when you see it, and to choose the kind of goals that excite you, that make more of you as a person. Do not give up on your dreams and desire, they are closer than you think, only a perception away...

ATTRIBUTES OF THE SUBCONSCIOUS MIND

As mentioned earlier on, we like to call the Subconscious mind your biological computer. For what could be more fitting to describe the part of you that is responsible to process millions of bits of information per second? It functions in collaboration with Source and Higher Self within you, and is responsible for absolutely everything to do with your physiological processes, insuring that all functions in perfect timing, the timing of Natural Intelligence. Your breath, your heart beat, your digestion, how your skin heals from a simple kitchen burn is run by your biological computer— your Subconscious mind. You can ultimately allow for healing in your own body as easily as you do for a kitchen burn or a small cut. Aside from making sure the cut is clean, it doesn't require any Conscious intervention such as any asking, praying, manipulating or intervening in any way. In fact, the less interference, the better. This is precisely what happens with spontaneous remission, and if allowed by the Conscious mind, would work equally well on most other physical illnesses you may have.

Just like a computer, your Subconscious mind replays faithfully all the programs that have been loaded into it, including your human genome, your family genetic and physical disposition and everything else you have picked up along the way, including what you have been telling yourself, and what you have absorbed from an external source.

The Subconscious is highly trainable, although the amount of time it takes for each individual may differ slightly. Remember how hard or how easy it was for you to learn how to drive a car, for example. Note how easy driving has now become for you. It takes absolutely no conscious efforts on your part, and you trust implicitly that you will know how to drive your car again next time you get into it. No doubt crosses your mind, your trust is absolute. In fact, while you drive, you even find yourself going over your day, or planning what you are going to eat when you get home. The planning is done with your Conscious mind, while your Subconscious mind—the one you trust implicitly— drives the car. We are saying this now because you will find this unshakable trust very useful when the time comes to trust the clearing taking place within you. Make a note here if you wish!

Unlike your Conscious mind, the Subconscious

mind never sleeps nor rests, it is active 24hrs a day, and only operates in the present moment. To put it simply, you, Dugast and everyone else would be long dead if it wasn't, as it handles millions of functions every second just to keep you alive.

Your Subconscious mind holds all programs that were ever put into it, and if you would like to extend your study, please do so as there is much material readily available on the subject. Our main concern is to give you a solution, and not get lost in too much more analysis of its functions.

Your beliefs and values are like a dial set on a thermostat—the Subconscious—which will remain so until you know how to change it. This also explains why, although you can 'breathe in' huge amounts of ever present raw potential, you can only configure that which you already know. In other words, you can only utilize that which you recognize through the bias of your beliefs and values. You can't know what you don't know. You don't see everything that is possible for you, you only see what you think is possible for you. A very big difference, and, in our experience, very, very, very far from your true capacity.

Your Subconscious mind is connected to your emotional body, which means that even if you don't consciously realize what kind of memories are replaying, you will certainly *feel* that something needs to be cleared, and will be able to use your tools. When it comes to clearing old programs, the less you figure out consciously, the better. You would only be adding extra layers of memories if you did, creating new stories, binds and locks, and getting lost instead of clear and free.

Best attributes of the Subconscious mind:
- ➤ One of the most powerful information processors known to Mankind.
- ➤ It reads the internal & external environment of the body and works to attune all internal systems accordingly, with the filter of previously recorded behaviors—programs—to determine a response. All of which is done with no help or knowledge from the Conscious mind.
- ➤ Processes more than 24 million environmental bits of information per second.
- ➤ Only abides in the present.
- ➤ Runs your biology and your Life, including all mental, physical and emotional processes and responses.
- ➤ Is highly trainable, and replays faithfully and endlessly all that is recorded within it.

Worst attributes of the Subconscious mind:

Just like a computer, it makes no difference between a program that benefits you, and one that keeps you stuck. It replays all faithfully and endlessly until the 'dial' on the thermostat is changed. This means that it is replaying all recorded events and memories from hurt/shock/trauma/limitations, some of them known to the Conscious mind, but most of them **are not known** and **can never be known** by the Conscious mind.

CONNECTING THE DOTS WITHIN THE MIND

Now that you have all the pieces laid out separately, let us reconnect them in their natural flowing order, which will allow the same to take place within you as you read it.

We have mentioned earlier on that 'A house divided cannot stand.' Beyond adapting this to the mind, it can also be adapted to external events as all reflect your internal state. This can also be experienced as a feeling of emotional disconnection, and exteriorly as fragmentation within your own family, your personal relationships, at work, etc. 'As within, so Without,' means that the division prevalent within the mind is reflected in outer circumstances, so you can recognize it and do something about it. We are simply describing the basis of what some of you prefer to call 'Quantum Physics.'

The fragmentation can range from mild to serious, and can be experienced as the 'insanity' quoted earlier. This internal 'split' means that, while the Conscious mind focuses on what is desired, often appealing repeatedly to a Higher Power, the Subconscious mind does the only thing it can: replay the programs that have been put into it. This means that your perceptions mostly remain the same, which is replaying the same kind of reality you have been living, including all problems and limitations if such is the case. This leaves very little chance for dreams and ambitions to manifest, causing extreme pain, self-devaluation and a loss of self-trust.

Simply understanding this can contribute greatly to alleviating much pain, and bring the renewed hope that everything is possible. It is! But we must say that no amount of awareness could clear this permanently, and no will power is strong enough to override a Lifetime of programs. If you know anyone who did it on awareness or will power alone, know that they are an exception.

CONNECTING THE DOTS
between
THE CONSCIOUS and SUBCONSCIOUS MIND

To allow these disparate parts of your mind to reconnect as a harmonious entity, your Conscious mind must first take some time to get acquainted with your Subconscious mind. The Subconscious has worked day and night for you, since you came into this physical existence, without ever being acknowledged, appreciated or sent any Love or gratitude. On the other hand, your Higher Self and Source in you, if you prayed, meditated or ever 'appealed to something greater than yourself', got all the attention and the Love. This is also why it seems impossible for some of you to Love who you are, which makes sense with such a enormous piece of yourself being left out.

So take some time aside, maybe 5-15 minutes, and either run with this mentally, or actually make a ritual of it if you want to. The essential element is that you finally address your Subconscious as a long lost part of you, for the first time in your Life. First acknowledge it, offer your heartfelt apologies, then proceed to ask for forgiveness. That part of you will grant you its forgiveness as it has been long awaiting your recognition and appreciation. Your Subconscious mind, just like your Conscious mind, is yearning to experience a freer Life with fewer limits. Please do this in a heartfelt manner, as you cannot fool your own vibration.

The reason for doing this is so that you fall in love with your Subconscious, ensuring that it falls in love with you—by you, we mean the Conscious aspect of you. You don't need to do this every time you connect with your Subconscious. Treat it as if you had just reconnected with a long lost beloved, and proceed as you would in real Life. If you went on making amends each time you met up, your beloved friend would ask you to 'move past this point, and enjoy a nurturing relationship!' Note, however, that making amends in the beginning is not only essential, it is vital. Only when this is done will you have the cooperation of the Subconscious, and the ultimate possibility to begin the clearing of the ties and binds that have kept you limited.

You must realize that your Subconscious is already in communication with your Higher Self, and that your Higher Self is always in a perfect working relationship with Source—Natural Intelligence. This is how you were created and how you keep breathing. Only the Conscious mind is left not knowing. Until now, your prayers, gratitude, Love or any other form of communication directed at non-physical aspects 'bigger than you' was addressed to your Higher Self, Source in you or Source outside of you, thereby ignoring the one aspect of you that is holding the Key to your freedom and transformation: Your Subconscious.

If you are serious about living a Life with fewer limits, accessing your fuller human potential, make the relationship between your Conscious and Subconscious mind a priority. Consider the Conscious mind the parent or the spouse to the Subconscious, and go about taking care of it, from today onward, as you would your own child or lover. We even suggest that this relationship take priority over all other 'worldly' relationships, as anything else you are involved with is a reflection and not a cause. This 'inner relationship' is one that will accompany you through space and time, unlike any other. When you will have done the initial reconnection, maybe several times, or until you feel it is established, you will want to name your Subconscious, or you will perceive a name. The name need not be a regular one, and can simply be a beautiful noun or word, as the aim of naming your Subconscious is to acknowledge that it is an entity in its own right, therefore emitting an energy signature. Even your pet has a name! Some pilots name their planes and some people their cars, so this is far closer to the truth than you ever suspected! If you are wondering if you could name your car, we say you certainly can! You will enjoy a better ride and have fewer breakdowns! We appreciate that this may sound unusual for some of you, while others may have already named their cars or trucks. Hence the 'identity' of all things as expressed in cartoons that some of your wiser Masters—your Children—watch.

Naming that powerful part of you will ensure that you will be able to address it directly, and release it from programs using thought form alone as you go about your busy day.

THE ORIGIN OF ANY PROBLEMS

Let explore where the problems really come from, since this is transmitted in reading format, which means you cannot ask direct questions.

Is there a problem with Source in you?

No, there is not. Source, being who you are at your Core—Natural Intelligence—is neutral and contains all creative potential. Being Pure

Abundance, it is wondering why you are asking for what you already have, and why you cannot hear the answers to your questions.

Is there a problem with your Higher Self ?

No there is not. Your Higher Self is in direct contact with Source in you, and together, they hold the Master plan for you, the overview. Your Higher Self holds your highest aspirations, and provides you with a constant stream of Inspiration in all its forms, for your ultimate wellbeing and thriving.

Until now, receiving Inspiration may have been a fleeting phenomenon, but when you know how to clear what is in the way, you will enjoy a streamline of Inspiration, or simply be able to access Peace of Mind anytime you wish to do so. Until now, the Conscious mind could only receive limited Inspiration, as it was often busy bombarding the Higher Self and Source with questions and requests.

Is there a problem with the Conscious mind?

Only in so far as it was ignorant of its inextricable relationship to the Subconscious, which meant it kept all blocks and limitations in place. However, with adequate practice and the willingness to let go at every occasion, it will be able to release the Subconscious from current and future programs, allowing clarity and freedom to prevail.

Is there a problem with the Subconscious mind?

Yes, as it is where all programs are recorded, kept in place by the conscious mind, which you experience as beliefs, limitations and problems. This means that the Subconscious was being treated as a slave by the Conscious mind. The Subconscious mind alone is not able to stop or alter any programs of its own accord. It needs the participation from the Conscious mind to release the inhibiting programs. You can compare the Subconscious mind with the hard drive of your computer, holding all data and programs, replaying all dutifully until you decide to go in and change them. As soon as the Conscious mind becomes aware of the Subconscious and begins a working relationship with it, you are on the road to freedom.

As you are consciously willing to drop ideas, beliefs and other thought-forms that create limitations, the Subconscious can instantaneously release the origin of the thought—the knot—that is causing the problem. The Subconscious mind, already working in perfect harmony to keep you alive and thriving, uses the same capacity to clear the emotional charge from problematic memories as it does to run your full biology. In other words, it is already connected with your Higher Self, which is itself connected to Natural Intelligence, which already orchestrates all with perfection and can transmute any problem. Now is the time to remember the analogy of the car, and how you can trust that you will be able to drive it next time you get into it. In the very same way, you can trust that, when you are willing to drop a problematic thought-form, it will be transformed. All you need to do is to let go.

Thought forms are energy, and energy cannot be created or destroyed but can be transmuted. This is the job of Natural Intelligence, your Creator.

Trust it.

It works.

SUBCONSCIOUS MIND ENTRAINMENT

It is the responsibility of the Conscious mind to train the Subconscious mind, so it can run the new clearing program, very much the same way that it runs all other programs. The way you train it, or 'download' this clearing program is by reading this manual several times, at least this chapter. When you feel it is done, it will be done. Once it is fully learned, it is recorded in your Subconscious. This is the same as learning to drive a car, it takes a little while before you do it 'automatically'. How long this takes really depends on you, and your level of commitment.

You will need to stay connected to your Subconscious daily, however. Hence the importance of having a name for it. This will allow you to express your love, your appreciation and gratitude directly to it. Moreover, knowing its name will allow you to directly communicate your willingness to drop limitations and fear-based thoughts as you recognize them. If you have a partner or family in your Life, we highly recommend you use the same attributes with them: love, appreciation, gratitude and willingness to drop what you know is not real or important. There is no end to how this practice can be adapted.

How to delete unwanted programs

Very simply by addressing your Subconscious by its name, let us say here that it is called Jade – this is the generic name offered during live Transmissions or until you get your own name—

and say, mentally or verbally:

'Jade, I release you from the anger that is in me right now,' or 'Jade, I release you from the feeling of expectation that is in me right now,' or any other challenge with which you are dealing. You can add, 'Thank you, I love you' as you consciously allow your Subconscious to drop programs. You can affirm your appreciation in any way that comes to you. There is no right or wrong, the important thing is that you are in close contact with your Subconscious, letting go at every occasion, expressing Love and gratitude as you go. This will become easier as you feel better in yourself and begin to see your Life change.

When there doesn't seem to be anything in particular that you can notice consciously, you can simply say 'I love you, I am grateful for your cooperation and our reunion,' or anything else that comes to mind and heart for you. Don't forget that you are only just beginning to clear layers upon layers of programs, so there is always something to clear, and as long as you live, you are being loaded with millions of bits of information per second. If you can't pinpoint what needs clearing, you can simply say or think:

'Jade, I release you from anything that stands

in the way of our complete Peace of Mind,' or 'Jade, I release you from anything that keeps us from absolute Love,' or 'Jade, I release you from anything that stands in the way of receiving absolute Abundance.'

Don't forget that you carry much that you are not consciously aware of, but has been accumulating since you were born and before with you family lineage. While this could be overwhelming, the way to clear it has never been easier, as it is done by using thought-form alone, the fastest and most powerful attribute known to Mankind. This doesn't take any time, space or any specific movement to work, hence its outstanding power and efficiency. If you are experiencing exhaustion or feel overwhelmed while reading this, we recommend you use your clearing tool right now:

'Jade, I release you from exhaustion and from being overwhelmed.' And it is DONE!

Some of you will respond to feelings rather than thoughts, in which case you can put your attention to your emotional body and check how you feel. It is easy to notice when you don't feel right. The challenge is bigger for when you feel good, as you can lose sight of staying connected and grateful, and forget your precious new step and your practice in general.

Say that you feel unable to make an important decision. The feeling behind this could be hesitation, or doubt, or fear of failure. In this case use:

'Jade, I release you from hesitation,' or 'Jade, I release you from doubt,' or adapt it to whatever is going on with you. You get the idea.

If you feel great and free and at peace, keep connected and express your Love and gratitude:

'Jade, I love you, I am so glad we are connected, I feel whole, I feel powerful while at the same time at Peace, and I thank you!' This is the space where your Life will begin to flow smoothly, when you will be in closer contact with the people you Love, receiving daily Inspiration and fresh ideas...something that will work for you at home, at work and while conducting business!

We fully appreciate that you cannot physically see the clearing taking place as it happens, especially in the beginning, but if you could, you would use it constantly! Not only does it take no space or time from your Life, it makes space for incredible things to happen in your Life. It makes you Miracle-prone! Be kind and patient with yourself, you deserve it.

Making sure your 'clearing download' remains active

So far, you have learned how to acknowledge your Subconscious, how to name it, and to address it so you are in close contact with it, moment by moment. The other main and last factor in this reconnection is the use of the breath. With Step One, you used the breath to come back to yourself, to stay aware and powerful throughout the day. Keep using that as your day unfolds, each time you are conscious of your breath, you are conscious! This allows you to become more aware of what is obsolete in your thought process and in your Life, which is why it is Step One.

Now we will also use the breath as the nourishment to let the Subconscious know that it is loved and cared for.

We would also like to make a useful comparison between breath and fuel. If you don't put fuel in your car, it will not go for very long. The same goes for your newly acquired relationship— reconnection—with your Subconscious mind.

It will stay strong and powerful if you treat it well, making sure you give it the fuel it needs to thrive: the breath. The breath is carrier of Air, the first and most important nutrient for your physical body. Water is the second nutrient, and food the last. While you can survive without water and food for some time, you can only live another few short minutes without breathing Air.

In the case of the Mind Triad, breath is the vehicle for energy storage, so it is vital that you use the following exercise.

Breathing Exercise

You can include this breathing routine morning and night, and for now, right after reading this part of the manual. If you meditate, it is a great tool to use before you start your meditation. This breath has been practiced in various forms by many of the most Ancient Traditions, and is best known as the Pranayama Breath by all meditation and yoga practitioners. It is adapted here for your convenience and to reflect your natural cycles.

Doing this breathing method will take about 3 minutes in the morning, and 3 minutes in the evening, so again, it is easy to integrate in the busiest of lives. If you ever have trouble going to sleep, you most probably will find that it will help. You can sit anywhere but make sure your feet are flat on the ground so you are connected to the Earth, benefiting from grounding and rooting energies. Keep your back comfortably straight.

The breath is as follows:
Do cycles of 3, 6 or 9 sets.
To begin with, you might like to use a cycle of 3.

- Have the palms of your hands open and facing upwards, resting on your laps
- Inhale to the count of 3
- Hold your breath to the count of 3
- Exhale to the count of 3
- And hold your breath to the count of 3

This is one round. Do as many rounds as the count of breath you chose, so if you started with 3, you will do 3 rounds, or 6 rounds if you chose a count of 6, etc.

THE SCIENCE OF LETTING GO

The easiest way to recognize what is going in you, what kinds of programs are running in your Subconscious when you are not conscious of it, is to note what emotions are in you. The emotional body is the expression of your Subconscious. It would be of tremendous value for you to realize what your 'default setting' is among all emotions. What we mean by that is that there are one or two predominant emotions that arise in you, with very little priming at any given time. This is why we call it your emotional 'default setting,' because it is the automatic emotional reaction that first comes up in you, even when you are not directly concerned.

For example, someone may get extremely angry very quickly for the smallest of reasons. You can see that anger was already there, below the surface, ready to rise at the slightest provocation. The emotion could be any other such as sadness, disappointment, blame, rage, etc.

Please take a moment now to examine what your emotional setting is (or are if you have more than one habitual response). You can even write it down.

These recurrent emotions are not going to be

dwelled upon or analyzed. As we have already said, *Connecting the DOTS* is not a therapeutic method. It is a Key to Freedom. You don't need to know what the emotion is tied to, or where it came from, and you don't need to bring up the story around it. All we propose is that you identify it, so that you will be able to release the first few big programs that are in you and holding you up. In fact, the less attention to the root cause the better. We hope this is a considerable relief for you.

Why not seek to understand the root cause of an emotions?

Why not? Because all things are a permanent echo; the results of an action, a word, a deed, an agreement or anything else that happened so long ago, that it is not possible to consciously get back to exactly when it started. Whenever you think it started, or why you think it started, was already the rippling effect and not the origin of the problem. Only your Subconscious knows where the knot is, and only Natural Intelligence can transmute it. These are the attributes that you already trust implicitly, remember? All the Conscious YOU has to do is to be willing to let go of what it perceives.

Attempting to untie a 'knot', which is the product of the Law of Cause and Effect, is not achievable by Man's Conscious mind, but an illusion that will cause many more problems, for generations to come. Man has created a lot of problems by now, making the need to include the Triad and Natural Intelligence in all things and living entities a priority. **The only real question is:** will you do it?

You are One, so each time you are willing to use your two steps, every-One and every-thing around you can benefit. This is a mathematical certainty, once again, sometimes called 'Quantum Physics.' All we say is that once you know what to do, you have a choice. This is your greatest privilege, and your responsibility.

CONNECTING the DOTS LOGO

This logo was drawn by Dugast in innocence as it was been 'doodled' years before *Connecting the DOTS* came together. It represents the United version of YOU.

Use it as you will, many have found it to have clearing qualities when included in paper work, contracts, travel plans, certificates, agreements, financial papers, creative projects, etc. It is the sum total and holds the same energy signature as the full book you are holding, which means that it contains the same transmitting quality for any-thing that it comes into contact with. Please see the note on page 149.

Answering a compulsion of perfectionism, Dugast tried to 're-draw' the logo several times since *Connecting the DOTS* entered the world in a public capacity, to which we made clear that it would lose all its frequency. We want to let you know that the same goes for you as we communicated to Dugast. While you can certainly photocopy the logo for your own personal use, and prove or disprove it effectiveness, physically duplicating it will reduce it to a 2-dimensional drawing, with nothing added unto it.

M. I. Dugast Ph.D.

CONNECTING the DOTS LOGO

88

CHAPTER THREE

QUESTIONS AND ANSWERS

Here are questions that have been asked during live Transmissions, and we thought you would enjoy them as you may be wondering about similar ones.

How will I know if this is working?

You will most certainly and gradually get a sense of Peace, increasing daily as you practice. Good or bad, all things are cumulative as you put your attention onto them. Before long, Peace of Mind will be the predominant order of the day, simply because you know how to deal with programs and repetitive thought forms, hard news or 'insurmountable challenges'. Step One ensures that you have each and every occasion to come back to yourself, and Step Two allows you to transform absolutely anything the moment you perceive it. You may begin to feel waves of quiet Invincibility! We highly recommend keeping a note of your progress again, as only then will you realize how far you have come since the beginning of your practice. You may even find that you have been upgraded from playing as an 'extra' in your own Life movie, to a Lead role!

What are beliefs and why would you would want to delete them?

A belief is simply a thought you keep thinking, either acquired from an external source, or born within you as a result of an experience. That doesn't mean it is true. Or it may be true for you, but not another. Your relationships can be a whole lot more enjoyable and far more transformative if each of you allows the other to be all that they need to be, marveling at each other's differences. Forcing your beliefs on another can have catastrophic consequences, or at the very least, make life dull for you and everyone else.

Cultivating unconditional Love, however, can make you enlightened.

Beliefs are made from thoughts and emotions, and become feelings. Feeling are the most powerful source of manifestation in you. They are described in your Scriptures as the Force 'that can move mountains'. Many Humans have killed to protect their own beliefs, or those of others. We invite you to be willing to let go of even your most cherished beliefs, which will allow you to become freer and allow you to see your Life and everyone in it in a whole new light. It will also allow you to receive the kind of Inspiration that will turn things around for you personally, and for your World.

Beware of the 'fear of lack of...,' which is a paralyzing feeling. Some of you have known real lack, but many haven't experienced it directly, but instead, as a family memory, which is still echoing and creating the lack of resources that may be currently experienced. You call it 'poverty consciousness.' The very thought of 'lack,' coupled with the emotion of fear, creates a feeling, the ultimate attractor factor. We recommend you get cleaning with all beliefs, as the inability to let go, no matter how subtle, keeps you imprisoned and impoverished.

Allow us to illustrate this predicament—the inability to let go—with a story many of you will have already heard. You may know about the monkeys that get captured without net or traps as such, simply because they reached into a carefully designed jar, which has a narrow neck. In order to run to freedom, which they would have ample time to do since they are not trapped, and run much faster than Man, they would have to let go of the handful of nuts to secure their freedom, but they cannot let go.

We recommend that you be willing to let go of even your best ideas, so the richness and abundance of Life can literally pour through you. Share your ideas, do not hoard them, they will grow and multiply, which will fulfil your sense of growth and contribution. You will enjoy true abundance! You have at your disposal, no matter what situation you find yourself in, access to the Intelligence that creates Worlds, so why would you settle for anything less?

Will the specific clearing I intended show up?

A word of caution here is to let go of wanting to see results in particular areas. Because Natural Intelligence takes care of transmuting your perceived problems, it will address what must be dealt with first. This may mean that something you hadn't counted on cleared before what you intended.

Your job is letting go, not hanging on.
Your assignment is Love, not control.

Remember that the origin of any problem is never what you think it is, you do not live long enough to see it with your Human eyes. Ties and binds are created with every breath you take, so we recommend you use your Steps, fall in Love with you and your Life, and have trust and fun in the process. This is about relinquishing control, not checking for results. The aim is a renewal of trust, the enjoyment of Peace and serving others using your gifts and talents. You live in extra-ordinary times, making History, and the quicker you can get into working in your area of contribution, the better it is for you, your family, and everyone else.

We are grateful to you. We Love YOU beyond words and reason.

Can I use these steps on other people and things?
You might like to go to page 149 as we addressed this question there. While wanting to

help others is a natural and beautiful tendency, we want to say to you that much gets done by taking responsibility to clear your own perceptions.

Now is the time to remember that you are One.

It is one thing to say it, but it will produce truly amazing results if you live it, trust it and use it.

Interference is never as good as taking responsibility. It is hard to re-wire yourself when you have been taught, probably all your Life, that changes are best made externally to be real and productive. We can assure you that it is not so. Nothing durable is achieved by external interference alone. The changes must take place within you first. All else can realign as you do, it is 'As within, so without.' It is basis of Quantum Physics. When you take care of working on you, every-One and every-thing can receive what they must, as all are linked to Natural Intelligence. When you interfere—a well-known human compulsion—you create friction, knots and further binds. This will probably take some getting used to, and some practice.

Remember, once again leaning on a science— Quantum Physics—you are familiar with: You live in an observer-participant World. You affect what you are looking at by simply observing it. You all share the same breath, walk the same ground, have the very same biology and share the same programs. You all want the same things. If you are privy to something that seems to be external, but is bringing up a strong emotion or reaction in you, it is most definitely something to do with you. It is a shared memory, it doesn't mean you did exactly what you are hearing or seeing. But it is YOUR chance to take responsibility for it in a unique way.

Because YOU are ONE, when you are willing to let go of it in you, to take responsibility to release it in you, you are undoing Eons of rippling effects, knots and binds that go back so far, you wouldn't believe it if you saw it. As you hear, feel, see and sense things and events around you that you perceive to be 'out of balance', or if things and events make you feel less than you now know yourself to be, all you have to do is to WORK on YOU. It is a beautiful thing. Freedom is at hand, for you and for All.

Remember that there is no boundary of space and time in reality, there is only the eternal moment. This means that the rippling effect of you taking responsibility to work things out of you sets a powerful clearing frequency that reverberates eternally. The energy signature you are sending out is one of Sovereignty, heralding the real possibility of a New Earth. This is why we said at the beginning of the book that your contribution matters beyond anything that can be expressed in words. It was not an 'empty' compliment meant for your ego, but an accurate description of the Power you really have, and how you can contribute to your World. In our humble view, there is nothing more important. The evolution and the thriving of your species depends on it.

Are there any good programs, and if so, how do I identify them?

Many programs and beliefs you are holding at present may be Life-enhancing and provide you with positive energy, which is a wonderful thing. Some aspects of your family lineage may indeed be best cultivated. So how do you identify good programs? Very simply by how they make you feel. Anything that affords you an expanded human capacity can be emulated by giving it gratitude. Feelings such as Love and any sub-division of the emotion such as courage, faith, forgiveness, determination, devotion, etc., can be emulated.

Anything that makes you feel less than who you are, such as doubt, self-pity, criticism, anger, resentment, etc., needs to be cleared out to make room for the real YOU. These are letting you know that there are programs in need of clearing.

In other words you can 'turn up the volume' when you feel an emotions to be Life-enhancing for you, or simply apply the 'delete' function when you know you must. Remember: attention energizes, while intention transforms.

I cherish some of my memories and do not wish to eliminate them... should I?!

First of all, let us reassure you and say that you will not go into any kind of amnesia as you are willing to let go of memories! Second the word 'should' has no place, not with us or anyone else!

Memories are holographic Life events that imprinted in your subconscious, according to the beliefs and values you had at that time. So proceeding to clear memories, good or bad, will simply allow the transformation—the transmutation—of the emotional-electrical charge that is attached to it. Applying Step Two will simply 'disengage' undesirable ripple-effects. Being willing to 'clear' a good memory will allow for everything to be as it must, and allow you and all parties concerned to feel what is yours more deeply.

The transmutation of memories will effectively

enable new perceptions to color an experience. You can quite accurately say that your willingness to let go and allow a memory to be transmuted by Natural Intelligence can literally 'change the past', including the Destiny of your 'future' family lineage in the process. We told you that you are far more powerful than you can imagine. This is just a glimpse of what you can achieve, which is phenomenal!

Do Inspired ideas need to be cleaned?

This is a very great question. We highly recommend that you do, as even the most wonderful of Inspiration, if not allowed to evolve organically, will turn into dogma and become unyielding, the opposite of evolution. Many concepts originally Inspired suffered this predicament in the hands of control.

So yes, we highly recommend that you use your Steps as you receive Inspiration. You will benefit by ending with a most refined version of it. This will also allow you to have what is truly yours, and allow everyone else to have the same.

Can you ask for specific things to be cleared out?

Once you commit to using these two Steps, we want to tell you that you had best delete the thought-form known as 'expectations', as these would otherwise literally stifle your success.

The Conscious mind usually wants explanations on how this works, how long it will take and when you will feel and see results. To the Conscious mind, this is what we say: the effect of each thought, word, deed and action that you, your family, relatives and ancestors have been involved in is as vast as it is unknowable because it is past. It started Eons ago, and has today rippled to your attention. Today, you are dealing with a particular set of repercussions—the Law of Cause and Effect—and, the best course of action we can recommend is what we have offered you with the two Steps given.

We highly discourage you from getting attached to when a particular problem will be cleared out, or how it will play out. One thing is certain: once you do the work, the work is done. Remember that limitations or exclusions imposed by the Conscious mind will only serve to create more knots and binds, new programs.

An excellent quality to emulate, which we consider no less than the ultimate heroic act of today, is to develop Trust. You only have to look at the sheer precision of way your Human body is 'engineered' to understand that it is a work of Art.

A simple biology class will serve as such a reminder.

Man, no matter how great an effort is made, shall never be able to accomplish what Natural Intelligence can do. This is a safety valve, Beloved One! Be glad for it! No amount of research with a particle accelerator or any other future machine being thought into creation as we speak will allow you to recreate how it all started. The Secret of Creation shall never be given to you to be replicated, not even to a group of you. The very best part you can play, more often than not, is to stay out of the way—Consciously speaking. The most productive state you can put yourself in is one of a student, marveling at Life. You have got to know that you don't know because you can't know. Be glad to practice, and enjoy your Life. It is a Gift.

Is it useful to name the rest of the Mind Triad?

One part of this Triad is already named by many and has caused much trouble and division among you, and throughout your World History. While you must proceed as you see fit to name the creative energy that is commonly known as 'God' as you see fit, it must not be a source of division. Remember that it is a natural compulsion for a Human to have Human compulsions! Beware however, of the 'judgment' program, which is rife among too many, and the root of much suffering.

Go ahead if you want to also name your Higher Self, but know that it has already been acknowledged with every transaction while you prayed or meditated, and therefore does not suffer from a lack of Love or recognition. Only your Subconscious has been left behind your whole Life.

What about my Angels and Guides?

There is absolutely no problem expressing your gratitude to your Angels, your Guides or any other Elementals or anything else you are accustomed to. However, if you are serious about wanting to live the kind of Life that has fewer limits, enjoy true freedom and access your gifts and talents, we propose you unravel your Human potential, which is often what you mistake for an external Entity. It is when you are willing to let go of ALL concepts and beliefs, no matter how wonderful, that the true blessings come. Have no fear, your contacts with what is will not disappear but rather be more profound, allowing you to enjoy the kind of adventure and miracles that can only come from non-attachment.

You are powerful beyond that which you can understand, and many times 'humanize' a gesture or state of Grace, as is a natural compulsion given that you are presently in Human form. We want to say to you that many a time, what you are experiencing is really the expanded version of you, following Natural Order. You have names for it like 'the parking Angel' for example, when synchronicity meets alert preparedness.

Remember that you are powerful beyond words, and even if this defies all understanding for now, we are confident that if you pay attention, while in the privacy of your own Being, you can certainly feel a glimpse of it deep down in you.

Now would be a great time to take a long, deep breath, and a few more if you will. A healing and a clearing of Self occurs as you do, bringing you closer to your own Abundant Nature.

What about prayers and wish lists?

Let's us address prayer first

Prayer is a frequency that is met by another frequency. In the pursuit of happiness, you often pray in lack and despair, in supplication, which insures that you get more of the same. The words may be kind and adoring, but you simply cannot fool your own vibration, which is the dominant attracting factor. We are talking here about very real energies and frequencies. Words do carry energy, but never as much as your own personal frequency. The other major thing, that can allow a shift or a breakthrough while you pray, is your breath. Breath is carrier of energy, which means it can freely flow from and to you.

When you wish to pray and make an offering of Love and Gratitude, know that your breath conveys it perfectly as it emanates your energy signature. You can use the breath given on page 82 to enhance your prayers. Begin by finding what you are truly grateful for, and follow by expressing your heart-felt gratitude for what is already on its way, as if it is already done. If anything comes in the way to detract from your prayer, use your Step Two. This is the frequency of manifestation, and is already used by a handful of you who do instant healing.

Anything you can sense, hear or speak out is already in a process of manifestation, which is why you have become aware of it. Let us use the analogy of a funnel for your Mind Triad, and say that the smaller end of it represents the Conscious mind. Meaning that, by the time you have become aware of something, it is already being manifested. [While this is a brilliant realization for a new business idea, it is far less pleasant for a cancer.]

Whatever you are dealing with, your job is to simply clear, or let go of, what is in the way—beliefs and limitations. This allows for all the pieces to fall into their right place at the right time, not 'your time' but Natural Intelligence's time, and, of course, take appropriate steps when you feel pulled to do so.

One more time, when you ask for something, it is already yours. Simply be grateful, and eliminate resistances. A good time to take another breath. A deep reconnection takes place when you do.

Regarding wish lists

There is much that you can miss when writing a wish list, as it is written from your Conscious mind, which is limited and loaded with programs. When you experience a moment of true Inspiration, you let yourself be carried by what is, not concerned with anything like a list.

Upon clearing your perceptions, you will probably find that many of your wishes are in fact programs you have absorbed along the way, which means that you can end up spending precious time and energy on something that is not really meant for you, or won't serve your growth or purpose as much as if you had simply eliminated all command.

Very simply, we recommend that you proceed with clearing what you perceive to be in the way, both in you and all around you, and the rest shall be added unto you. If you will just clear your mind and fall in love with the totality of who you are, you will achieve much while staying connected.

We want to make a distinction between wishing and designing from Inspiration, which are not the same. Wishing often means that there will be little or no need to take action on your part, while receiving Inspiration will naturally precede a goal or plans to achieve something, and is therefore understood to require your absolute and active participation. Your physical body has, among others, two main purposes. The first is that it is a delineated boundary with which you can experience contact with things and people in your Life. The second is that it is the vehicle that allows you to take action when you feel Inspired. You may be surprised to hear how so many people have wishes but do absolutely nothing to manifest them. For example, wishing to become financially rich while sitting idle in their house, or wishing to lose weight but not being willing to take a simple daily walk, or wanting to meet the love of their Life without venturing out in any shape or form. We know this sounds foolish but it is often the case.

We invite you to follow this simple recipe, which is to state clearly what you want to accomplish or experience—write it down. As you make **every effort** to move in the direction of the desired goal or plan, use your Steps One and Two to recognize and clear what is in the way. The clearing of obstructions is the element that makes all the difference.

If you are going to ask for something, we propose that you develop the art of asking empowered questions, so you can receive empowering answers. All of the asking is best done within you only, and can be applied to any situation, personal or external. These are:

Is there anything I am not hearing?

Is there anything I am not sensing?

Is there anything I am not doing?

You will certainly receive some cues as you stand alert and united within. To your success!

Do I need to use affirmations?

Everything has its time. While you can, of course, still use affirmations, make sure that you take the Inspired step, the ACTION that will allow whatever you are affirming to manifest. Otherwise, not much can happen.

Do not use future tense with your affirmations as this keeps it in the future and therefore permanently unreachable in present, real time. Avoid using words like 'trying,' 'hopefully' or anything similar as this pertains to a third party having power over you, disabling you from your own resolves and decisions. Remember that judgment only exists in the mind of Man.

Remember that an idea is simply the not-yet-manifested version of your dreams, plans and goals. It is nonetheless already done, which is the only reason why you are perceiving it in the first place.

Inspired ideas do not come from you,
but through you.

The fun of it is to play your part in seeing it unravel in a physical, manifested form. You are the lucky participant of Creation in motion. You can accurately say that each of you is a Master Alchemist!

When will I be free?

The potential for you to begin living a Life

where the Peace within prevails, meaning that you have attained personal freedom, is very real if you will simply practice Steps One and Two. While 'success' means different things to many of you, we propose that Peace is the best foundation for whatever type of success you want to experience.

However, to address the question as to when exactly you should feel this solid Peace of Mind, we can only say that it very much depends on your level of practice and self-discipline. This is no exception to any other new technique you might wish to learn, and, just as if you were starting to practice a new sport, or learning to play a new instrument, you wouldn't expect to excel at it straight away, and not without daily practice. The very same applies here. If you are experiencing feelings such as doubt, expectations, impatience: these are the programs that you can simply clear out, using your Step Two.

By the time your mind works as a Triad, in dynamic partnership with Natural Intelligence, you will find that compulsive thought-forms such as 'impatience' or 'doubt' do not serve any purpose. The best option for you to feel freer more quickly is to simply 'delete' them, using your Step Two.

Is *Connecting the DOTS* the same as other therapies that deal with clearing Subconscious programs?

Connecting the DOTS is not at all a therapy but a way of Life; a way to get yourself free, not simply better. It is wonderful, however, that many therapies can reach the Subconscious and help to eliminate patterns. If you presently use such therapies, you will find that *Connecting the DOTS* works in the background of what are practicing. This is because it is designed to work on YOU directly, which means it cannot and does not need to be shared or explained to anyone. **It is for you.** Remember, you are One. So if you do the work within you, it gets done externally, including in your clients, your children, your spouse, etc.

It is as efficient as it is unobtrusive, as there is nothing faster than thought-forms, faster than even sound or light. With practice and the daily use of the breath given to train and nurture your Subconscious, the clearing will even take place while you are asleep.

Connecting the DOTS is vastly different from any therapy because the two Steps given do not require that you lean on anyone else. It is something that can be practiced with your own resources, not requiring any special physical gestures or any specific location, giving you a way of accessing permanent Peace of Mind. Unlike the aim of therapy, we are not looking to get over anything, but rather to get into everything that you ever wished to experience, making you more resourceful, able to face anything what comes you way.

Will all my fears and problems disappear?

Having Peace of Mind and living a fear-less Life does not mean that all your problems will disappear. New problems and limitations may come in, as they play many roles. A driving force for some of what you are experiencing is your natural impulse to keep on evolving, so you can become more of who you truly are. It is less about avoiding problems, and more about becoming all that you can be. Eventually, problems will avoid you!

You can believe us when we tell you that we know what you are capable of because we can see it, having a certain 'overview,' and we say that you haven't even grazed the paintwork yet!

What about using mind-reprogramming technologies?

Don't ever forget that you have free will. You

must do what you feel you must do. The best course of action is to use your two Steps, and direct all your questions inwardly, and do what feels right for you. However, since we are here together for now, we will answer one last question.

There is much—and will be increasingly more—in the way of technology that is created to 'reprogram your mind'. Readily available to buy commercially are programs such as self-trust, Love, success and many other positives ones. We would just highlight the fact that recording new programs over old ones doesn't insure that the former ones will not resurface. We like to use the analogy of the tapes you used to use—if you are anywhere near Dugast's generation—and that if you ever recorded a piece of music on a used tape, you would remember that the sound would be clear for a time, but at some point, you would hear the old piece of music underneath the new one. If you are going to use mind reprogramming technology, we would recommend that you do so after using the two Steps given here. You will have better success if you do, and perhaps even find that you do not need reprogramming after all, as you have already have a natural inbuilt version, that gets updated as you breathe!

What about the use of nanotechnology in medicine and Human potential?

Yes, nanotechnology is being 'perfected' and will shortly be used as a means of treatment in medicine, and sold as a way to achieve Peace of Mind, and accessing your expanded Human potential. We urge you to remember that any-thing that is created is an Entity, with the same Mind Triad as we have described, and also is connected to Natural Intelligence. You will therefore continuously benefit from using your Steps, which will allow you to make the best and most educated choices for yourself.

THE EVOLUTION OF MANKIND

You are living during crucial times, and we want to highlight the fact that, by now, you have a choice. The thriving and the continuous organic evolution of Man very much depends on the diligent application and respect of your Natural and Physical Laws. Much needs to transform, and, as you already know, the best chance you have to make a real difference, no matter where you contribute in your Society, is to change your present mind-set, no matter how advanced it may be at this point. It can and must be allowed to be more advanced yet. As you already know, the same mind-set will only create increasingly complex predicaments. The best tools at your disposal today is accessing your Higher Mind, the main frame computer if you prefer more scientific terms. This is done upon practicing the Steps we gave you, or any other you may already be practicing, that contribute to the same outcome: your freedom, and the expansion of your potential, so you share the gifts you came to share. There is something very precise you are here to do, and the quicker you find what that is, the better your Life will be, and everybody else's too. You are One.

The time has come for ALL of you to prosper,

so it is vital that you allow yourself to share your specific skills, without censoring or judging them to be 'not important.' They are, and you are. You deserve every encouragement to be all that you can be. We sincerely hope that you have received all that we gave you here in the best possible of way, as it is Transmitted in LOVE.

Many surprises are on the horizon, among them, the complete turn-around of what you still call today your 'third world countries.' These will rise to unprecedented new standards, and will be the place where many of you will want to be, to participate in a flourishing economy, abundant in resources and producing many sought-after products and new Naturally-based Technology. May we remind you, at a serious risk of sounding repetitive, that any-thing that is creation has a Mind Triad, and is a part of Natural Intelligence. Let that be your clue for any place, any country, any-thing you can think of!

As you know by now, the Subconscious is loaded, every fraction of every second, with new data, amounting to millions of bits of information per second. While we don't wish to overload you, we consider that forewarned is forearmed, and therefore want to tell you that these millions of bits of information are about to increase exponentially as you go on developing the technology of Communication. The technology of Communication is the real power and currency of your Era, based on thought-forms. Communication is the Power that will ultimately revolutionize your present World, if used correctly and with foresight. And again, there is much that you are not using at present, but you will begin to do so within a few decades.

Following the model of duality, there will also be other kinds of technology, perhaps less desirable, that may be less complimentary to your Human free will. You will be very glad to have a 'cleaning download' at your own disposal, within your own biology, for we can promise you that these will not age, but only get more refined with practice.

REVISING THE TWO STEPS

Step ONE: Come back to awareness as often as you can throughout each day, using your pointers—your list of things that bug you or delight you. Practice was never made easier! Use the breath to reconnect with your Core Self throughout the day.

Step TWO: Once you have made the initial reconnection with your Subconscious mind, give it a name that honors it. Every day, acknowledge it and treat it like the beloved part of you that it is, loving it so much that it has no other choice than loving you back. It will then be onboard to clear all programs, even while you sleep. Use the specific breathing method given twice a day, upon rising and before retiring. This is to fuel the Subconscious with necessary energy, nourish it and train it. Use 'I release you from...'at any occasion and when you encounter problems, difficulties and blockages. Or when you feel everything is wonderful, to feel more peace, more inspiration, more love and more gratitude. As you do, you will be radiating all these qualities and your Presence will grow.

CHAPTER FOUR

CONNECTING the DOTS OVERALL

There is nothing more for you to practice in what you will learn in the following chapter. However, it will allow you to understand how you function as a whole, which can potentially free you as you read it, and allow for all kinds of Miracles to take place in your physiology.

It will also enable you to understand the real process of manifestation, from the most minute and internal, at the quantum level, all the way to the larger externally manifested reality. From the microcosm to the macrocosm.

YOUR QUANTUM ANATOMY

THE SUM OF ALL PARTS

The *User's Manual To Being You*

Forgive us for this analogy if you don't find it humorous—we certainly do!—but even when you buy a frying pan, there is a User's Manual. So we thought it a timely gift to come up with a manual for YOU, the magnificent Creation that you really are.

YOU are CO-CREATOR

0
GOD
SOURCE
THE VOID
GREAT SPIRIT
THE KINGDOM
NOTHINGNESS
PURE POTENTIAL
DIVINE INTELLIGENCE
MAGNETIC / NATURAL INTELLIGENCE
(The Owner)
↓

MENTAL
(The Manager)
HOUSE OF SELF
(Super-Conscious, Conscious, Subconscious)
IDEAS
(Inspired/Programmed = Seed)
↓

EMOTIONAL
(The Navigation system GPS)
FILTER
(Glue/Soil= Sorting office)
↓

PHYSICAL
(The Vehicle)
MANIFESTATION
(Growth/Embodiment/Calcified thoughts)

ALL MEN ARE CREATED EQUAL

We have allocated many possible names to Natural Intelligence, the same intelligence that creates Worlds, as this Manual is intended for everyone. So whether you prefer to know yourself as 'Pure Potential', or as 'Incarnated Divine Intelligence' or as 'Nothing-ness,' one thing is for sure: you have a mental body, an emotional body and a physical one. This illustrates the accurately famous statement originally coined by Thomas Jefferson "All men are created equal." The only difference is that the disconnection is such in some, that it wreaks havoc through illness and limitations pervading the mental, emotional or physical body.

The Owner – Natural Intelligence

As you can see, we have arranged Natural Intelligence to be at the top of the diagram and we call it 'the Owner.' This is because it is *that* which gives you the breath. It ultimately holds all creative attributes and possibility for Mankind, and can transmute any kind of energy. **It is the only One to have such attributes.** If certain sciences and approaches used today still experience limitations, it is due to the simple fact that the Owner—Natural

Intelligence—is discounted, leaving an enormous part of any problem—and therefore the solution—out of the equation. The same goes for technology and all that are perceived as 'inanimate' objects. Each and every molecule at the base of any creation contains Natural Intelligence, which means that anything that simply 'is,' is a live entity.

In total, there are only two kinds of creation in your World, what you call 'God' made, or simply the Natural Kingdom, and all other creations which are Man-made. Both are intrinsically intertwined, but the perceptions emitted by most people right now still contribute to cementing the compartmentalization between spirit and matter, between you and all 'things.' This results in the exponential division of the Life-force available to you and, because you are One, to everyone else. Greater progress and results can and will be made upon including The Owner in all encounters, transactions and exchanges, whether you are dealing with people or 'inanimate' objects.

The Manager – Your mental body

We have called the mind as a whole, the MANAGER. This Manager is the tool that allows you to make choices, and, paired up with emotions, gives you the creative ability to put into motion what you receive in the form of ideas. It is also your cognitive tool, and has many other functions already explored with Step One and Step Two.

For many who are at the mercy of their mind, however, the Manager is often mistaken for the Owner. This means that the mind is all ruling, and that the person in question is at the mercy of their mind: a dangerous place to be. The ideal situation is that your mind is at your service, and not the other way around. We explored the ego mind with 'Attributes of the Conscious Mind' in Chapter Two. Personal crisis usually hits, giving a chance to allow for re-prioritization and to find out what is real and what is not. Although this is not always recognized as such, a crisis is really an opportunity in disguise, here to enable each to wake up to their fuller potential and to realize that there is Intelligence beyond the mind.

We also call your mental body the HOUSE OF SELF, which we explored with Step Two, as it is made of the Higher Self, the Conscious Self and the Subconscious Self. We want to highlight that your mind is not in the brain, but is in every cell in your body, all hundred trillions of them. Your brain is simply the antenna which responds to what the mind is feeding it, setting neurotransmitters into motion, manifesting all from your internal biology to your external and perceived reality. The brain doesn't know if what is taking place is real or simply imagined—projected mentally. Much of this is common knowledge and is used as mind conditioning by athletes, during the Olympics, for example, where they 'see themselves' winning in advance. It works. Success is opportunity meeting preparedness.

We invite you to review what you usually project for yourself, as it is contributing to your perceived reality and what you can manifest...or not. Natural Intelligence is present in each and every one of your cells, which means that there is a full mind in each and every one of your cells, making all Miracles possible. Once again, all that is required is that you clear what you perceive to be in the way in the form of beliefs and opinions—programs—and allow the bigger part of you to do its work.

The mental is where the SEEDS of all creations incubate, in the form of IDEAS. Your mind responds to only one of two Masters at any given time, either Inspiration or programs (see diagram on page 137). Some ideas are Inspired, and some are programs. Some are programs passing as Inspiration. If you are not sure of what you are hearing, it would be called 'doubt'. You would first have become aware of what is going on within you, with your Step One, and immediately put Step Two into action; in this case by thinking or saying to your Subconscious mind 'I release you from doubt.'

Any of the programs you carry (millions of layers) have mostly been fed to you by an external source, even if they came from well-meaning parents, school, society, etc., or born within you as a result of comparison, or any other fear-based thought such as competition, judgment, fear of lack of...,fear of being judged, fear of not being enough, fear of not being Loved, etc.

We want to give it to you in a simple mathematical equation:

You + Natural Intelligence = Success in all things
You − Natural Intelligence = Limits and hardship

Remember that, for each limit that you recognize consciously, there is a multitude that remains unconscious, but is none the less active and playing the major role in shaping your reality. Some of the things you hold so dear are really only someone else's thoughts and perceptions, still echoing in you. This is why, among the many cosmic Laws that resurfaced in recent years, the Law of Attraction got the most popularity. While the Law of Attraction is very real, there are many other Laws at play. We must make a major distinction, however, and say that you attract with your full vibrational frequency, and not just with your Conscious thoughts and directed emotions. Your vibrational frequency is largely shaped by your emotional body, which responds to the signals and programs that are running within your Subconscious mind. These keep running as formerly instructed, until you begin to clear your perceptions. In other words, you do not attract so much consciously as you do subconsciously. What you attract is what is really going on within you that you need to see—so you get a chance to clear it—and not exclusively what you want Consciously. Hence the things and events that come into your Life unannounced, that you definitely did NOT ask consciously to experience.

Life is your most powerful Teacher, here to remind that most things are beyond your control. Your wisest approach is one of awareness, and of willingness to let go. You have each and every way of doing that by now. Our upmost loving concern is that you live at Peace, remaining clear, alert, stable, resourceful and powerful, manifesting the gifts that are yours to give.

The Navigation System GPS – Your emotional body

Your emotional body is essentially a vibrational translator actively configuring and processing information from your five senses, and all your other subtle energy receptors, such as the heart and your energy fields. It is your inbuilt 'inner compass' that lets you know what kind of thoughts you are harboring, both conscious and unconscious.

The emotional body, as you can see on the diagram, is also called the GLUE, the SORTING OFFICE and the SOIL. All of these pertain to illustrating the connective element that the emotions represent. The emotional body is the deciding factor that determines what is possible for you and what is not.

We call it the GLUE because without the emotions, no thought can manifest. This affords you a good amount of Peace, as you may have recently revisited some age-old thoughts that are not at all congruent with what results you wish to see in your Life.

We call it the SOIL, because there is another Law which is not spoken of very often, yet a crucial element to the manifestation process: The Law of Germination. It is also known as the Law of Incubation or Gestation, depending on the subject. You are familiar with the Law of Germination, for example, while growing plant food, the Law of Incubation when you think of an egg which will hatch into a chick, or the Law of Gestation when you think of a Human embryo developing into a baby. The same Laws apply to all ideas. We see much impatience amongst you, wanting to get everything done faster and faster, to acquire things and results, but the truth of the matter is that the span of time it takes for a thought to come to fruition in its physicality is not only essential, according to the Law of Gestation, it is actually a luxury for you.

We call it this luxury the 'buffer of time,' for it is a gift, affording you time to 'change your mind,' or clear your thoughts. Why do we say this? Because if every thought you behold manifested instantaneously, I think you will agree that you—and Dugast both!—would be in big trouble! This

Law gives you a chance to change your mind, hence leaving you a 'window of time' during which your feelings can change, allowing different results to manifest. We want to tell you that this gift will not always be so. Right now, you are given some 'training time' so you can get used to understanding and practicing how this really works. This is a good thing, because there will come a time when the manifestation process will be much faster, even faster than it has become in the recent years, leaving you less room for mistakes. You are learning how to mind your own frequency, and this 'buffer of time' is giving you a chance to do just that.

In fact, the manifestation process will become so much faster, that it will take days where it used to take months, minutes and seconds where it used to take days. Some of you are already working in this capacity, but not most people. We are talking here of Natural manifestation and not Man-made creations, as has already happened, altering the natural cycle of many natural elements, which is causing many problems and many more binds. Yet another opportunity to clean with perceptions...

As you may already know, there are places on your Beloved Mother Earth right now, where the span of time between thought and manifested reality is much shorter than in other places. This calls for people who can 'mind their frequency,' a very big responsibility, and a good training ground.

We call it the SORTING OFFICE because the kind of creation that is being shaped really depends on the nature of the emotion. Most of the time, you only realize just how powerful or devastating an emotion really is when you see its physical, manifested aspect. This was certainly the case when Dugast was finally diagnosed with cancer. Although the cleaning of thoughts and perceptions on the subject began upon receiving the pre-cognitive diagnosis, the original thought form paired up with the emotions still proceeded to carry the manifested illness to visible terms. Seeing the opportunity to apply *Connecting the DOTS* to the occasion, Dugast was a witness to spontaneous remission within a few months. We are here to tell you that this is accessible to anyone, as you are all created equal, and are One.

To sum it up in a simple format, you will remember that negative emotions compress your DNA, causing illness, faster aging and other serious problems; while positive emotions enhance your DNA, allowing you to expand, regenerate and rejuvenate, literally. Spontaneous remission in itself is the result of an increase in DNA.

While there is much talk and fascination with increasing your DNA on command, we want to tell you that, if you simply take care of staying at Peace and in Love, clearing programs and limitations within you, your DNA will naturally increases. And, as you may have guessed, faster than what you could imagine. You don't need to ask for it to increase, it is already yours and part of the natural process unfolding within you as you choose to let go and let live.

We are not suggesting for a second that you should force yourself to stay positive, because if you have tried, you will have noted that it is quite impossible. There is an ebb and a flow that belongs to all Life forms, and just like the tides of your seas, your emotions fluctuate. You are no exception, being the precious 'Natural Phenomena' that you are! You can simply use your two Steps to clear the programs and patterns that are in the way of your contentment, peace and potential, all already within you. As you release what comes up, a long lineage of family history gets cleared up, and you naturally have access to more of who you are.

Emotions are your NAVIGATION SYSTEM,

otherwise known as your inbuilt GPS. They let you know via your intuition, seated at your solar plexus, what is going on around you in a vibrational capacity. You have walked in places before where 'the feeling' or 'the vibe' was so bad that you had to make a quick exit. This is very much following your inner guidance, your 'in-tuition,' as true guidance is never wrong. The challenge is to recognize the mind when it comes in to rationalize an otherwise perfectly good signal from your GPS.

The Vehicle – Your physical body

Primarily, your physical body is your vehicle, a boundary within which you can experience your human existence. As duality would have it, however, the fact that you are embodied in an individual shape also gives you the illusion that you are on your own, which is not the case. Honoring this can alter how you see others for the better, and what you are willing to do or say to another, when you realize they really are a part of you.

We call the body CALCIFIED thoughts, because you get to see what you have been thinking, and what you have been feeling in a physical, manifested form. Your physical body and your present reality are the sum total and the product of this mechanism. The state of your body is never static in its nature, but is the manifested expression of the information it receives, both from the mind-emotions chemistry, and the environment. It is in a constant state of fluctuation. As you breathe, the energy received is transmuted into information, allowing a certain reality to take place, reflecting your personal beliefs and values. Once again, your programs.

In other words, you shape what is possible and what is not possible within your own biology with each breath you take. You also shape what experiences can come into your Life in the same way. This is both conscious and subconscious, hence our dedication to enabling you to *Connect the DOTS* with us.

THE SUM OF ALL PARTS

You are made of the sum total of these four elements: Core, mind, emotions and physical. First, you are Core—Natural Intelligence—whether this is acknowledged or not. Then you have mind, fuelled with inspired thoughts or programs, both conscious and unconscious. Thoughts filter into your emotional body, develop as feelings and give shape to the last stage of manifestation which you experience in physical, tangible terms. This applies both to your own biology, determining the state and health of your body, and to your external perceived reality, your experience of Life. This is why we call the physical body and your manifested reality 'calcified thoughts,' as you get to see what you have been thinking and feeling: an incredibly precise Design...Of course, the word 'calcified' does quite reflect the true natural of physicality as 'calcification' evokes a kind of immovable solidity, which is not accurate as any physical manifestation is only as 'real' as the perception of the Observer. It will change as you change. However, it becomes 'calcified' enough for you to take note of it and act accordingly. A beautiful and generous mechanism.

Mind Revolution: Communal Thinking

The sum of all parts that we have just described applies to each and every one of you cells. **This is worth repeating:** these four elements: Natural Intelligence, and the mental, emotional and physical aspects are the same elements that make up each and every one of your cells. All hundreds of trillions of them.

Take a breath to get out of the head and allow this

information to resonate with the deeper part of
you, a healing of Self occurs as you do.

This means that each cell has its own intelligence, and that it doesn't work as a singular entity, but rather as a WHOLE, as a community. You cells respond both to the environment they live in, and the thoughts that you emit—your beliefs. This literally imprints your DNA and shapes your biology, and your World at large. And, you will have guessed it by now, this will also change as you change your thinking. All the Conscious YOU has to do is to simply clear what is in the way, and you know exactly how to do this by now.

There is little to no hereditary factor imprinted within any of your cells. The only hereditary factors, if you want to call them that—we prefer the term 'contributing factors'—is the thoughts and the words you repeat, and the environment, all of which are picked up by cell receptors, which charge the cell with a particular command—an imprint. There is nothing pre-destined in your cells.

In other words, you can think yourself into health, no matter what you have been told is hereditary in your family lineage. This also means that any other perceived 'lack' or trait of character you 'thought you inherited' is only as real as you want to keep it. The only true hereditary factors are thoughts: the story you keep telling yourself. We trust that you appreciate the positive ramifications this has for you, your family, relatives and ancestors, and your World at large.

Now is a good time for a deep breath, to allow the information to penetrate each and every one of your cells. A healing occurs as you do.

This process is described extensively by some of your leading neuroscientists as a branch of science called 'Epigenetics' and, as always, you can study much more about it, or join us at a *Connecting the Dots* Transmission. In the meantime, you have your Steps, the essential and practical part you can play in your own Life right now. We invite you to move from the intellectual receptor to your body Intelligence using your breath.

The miracle mind of cellular community
The fact that each cell has its own intelligence explains the miracles that many have encountered, often in being told that a part of their body would never work again, only to prove the contrary within

months, and sometimes weeks or even days. As already mentioned, the mind is not in the brain, but in every cell. This mean that each cell is able to 'think' for itself as it is connected to the rest of the community—the other millions of cells, and to you, the Host, representing its environment. The best you can do is to remain at Peace, in Love and Laughter. What this really means is that there is no end to what Natural Intelligence can realign within you, once the limitation of the mind is out of the way, and again, you know exactly how to do that with your Steps One and Two.

Practicing these two Steps will allow you to be the instrument of your own Miracles, no matter what you seek. What you call Miracles, we call Technology, the Technology you now know, as described in *Connecting the DOTS*.

A DIAGRAM-SUMMARY OF YOU AND YOUR CELLS

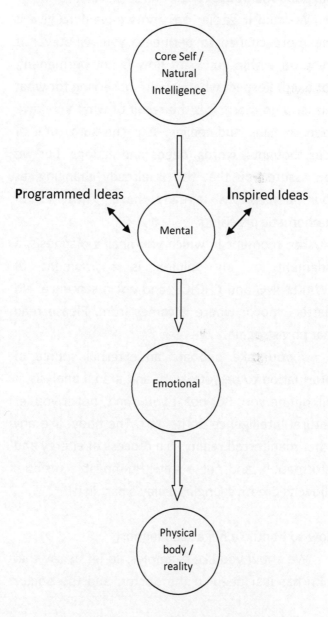

The diamond in the rough

We said it earlier on, and we want to give it one more chance to permeate you: whatever is going on within you right now is not permanent, not fixed. Respect what you are observing for what it is, and no more: it is the result of what you have been thinking and feeling. It is the sum total of your thoughts, words, deeds and actions, but we can assure you that this is already changing, as your perceptions already have. This is of mathematic precision.

The moment in which you hear a diagnosis, a judgment or an opinion is a moment of AWAKENING and CHOICE, and not a sentence. No matter who or where it comes from. Please read that phrase again.

If you take onboard an external source of information to be your truth and a final analysis, it will define you. But not if you don't; not if you let Natural Intelligence do its part. The body, like any other manifested reality, is a process of energy and information, and not a static, immovable residue. Allow its Creative Origin to play a part in it!

How to handle a negative diagnosis

We know you like examples, so let us say that John has just been to the doctor, and the doctor said to him that he has a form of cancer, quite advanced in its development. We can hear you ask what kind of cancer he has, and we can tell you that the kind matters not. The cause, however, is always the same: the emotions of fear and the feeling of entrapment that goes with it. Fear—and all its sub-emotions—is at the root of all your illnesses, and the cause of premature death, save for accidents and the natural end of your physical journey.

Back to John. What the doctor is describing— unbeknownst to himself due to his specific training—is the result of fear-based thoughts, both conscious and unconscious, and/or the environment that John lives in.

John may in fact have been aware of deep seated fear, fear of loss, anxiety, fear of illness or he may have exposed himself to daily stress with his job or at home. In the latter case, he may have opted to numb out the pain with overwork, alcohol, TV, gambling, or any other addiction in the attempt of getting some momentary relief. Or perhaps he wasn't aware of anything in particular and just felt depressed, living the kind of dull existence he thinks everyone lives.

Whether conscious or unconscious, his thoughts certainly messaged his emotional body, which in turn imprinted his cells, finally manifesting as cancer in his physical body. The manifestation of cancer here is the illustration of the crisis discussed earlier, the opportunity to address what has been ignored, and the invitation to become whole, to come back to the true, Core Self, and to change something about the way things have been handled until now. Sometimes it heralds the end of one's physical existence, of course, which cannot be redeemed. The Steps will bring Peace to prepare for such a Journey. Often, however, it is the product of living a Life out of balance.

Now pay attention!

Here is the GIFT: the process described above has taken an amount of time to develop, which, by the way, doesn't mean that it will take as long to resolve itself. Do you remember the 'buffer of time' we discussed earlier on? Well, this is now going to serve John. The diagnosis offered is a description of the thoughts-emotions-physical process. It is not a final or static reality. It is a thought that has 'calcified enough' for John to see it, but not calcified to the point that it cannot be changed. The outcome, following John's meeting with his physician, depends on John's state of mind, and his ability to understand it for what it is: either a death sentence, or the sum total of John's Life and the opportunity to change something in it. The operative message here is CHOICE.

Other creations follow the same model

Let's say that you want to create a work of art, change something in your business or write a book. Whatever it is, it follows the same model of creation. First, there is thought—inspired or not. Second, there is the emotions for the project—the fuel of creation. Third, there is physical manifestation and the actual steps to make it tangible.

The crucial and defining factor is to be willing to 'clean' even your best of ideas. This means that you will allow them to be all that they can be, meaning you will allow them to be imbued with Natural Intelligence. Holding on to anything—even ideas—in a tight grasp will not allow for anything fresh to be added unto them.

Making good use of your emotions

As we say earlier on, your emotions are the essential connectors in your manifestation process, either alerting you to what need to be cleared, or giving you a chance to emulate a quality. An easy way to identify what to keep or clear is as follows. Your positive emotional range produces the most creative energies and the highest biochemistry regeneration available in your body, which naturally allows your DNA to unfold—meaning that you are tapping into a more robust version of you. As you do so, your reality will match your inner state, bringing unprecedented possibilities into your Life.   This positive emotional range begins with LOVE, and all its subcategories, such as trust, faith, joy, abundance, generosity, gratitude, etc. These create the perfect environment for outstanding health, including when you are at Peace, feeling contented. This is the space that allows for all good things and many Miracles—big and small—to be recognized in your Life.

The other emotions are the ones that often herald a crisis—an opportunity to change—and are based on FEAR and all its sub-categories, such as: addictions, guilt, criticism, anxiety, self-doubt, anger, self-hatred, judgment, comparison, competition, etc. Any of these emotions felt on a daily basis provide the soil, the ground on which illnesses of all kinds can manifest: mental, emotional or physical, and in more extreme cases attempt to shut down one's biology, which shows up as potentially fatal illnesses and premature death. By the time any kind of crisis shows up, it has gone through the process of Incubation via sustained thoughts and emotions, which, remember, are not static but rather a distress signal for you to change course. It is only on a very few rare occasions that it heralds the end of the journey; in which case both Steps can still be applied to move into a graceful and peaceful state before entering non-physicality.

For the most part, a crisis comes in as an ally, providing a warning to allow for change, either with the inner dialogue, or the environment that you live in, or both. The intensity of the perceived adversity varies with how hard a jolt is needed for change and awakening. This can range from mild to severe, but always providing an opportunity to remember who you really are and what you came here to be and do, enabling you 'crack open' to Light.

What about stress?

Just remember that, physiologically speaking, when you are suffering from stress, it means that your body is flooded with the 'fight or flight' adrenaline response designed to enable you to react to danger. You are built in a way that is meant to sustain this 'fight or flight' response for short periods of time ONLY. Allowing stress to run through your body on a daily basis will shut down your biology prematurely, sooner than later. If you are prone to serious stress, we highly recommend that you practice your Steps many times throughout the day, which will become automatic once in learned memory. If you find it useful, set your phone with reminders. Practicing your Steps diligently will literally save your Life, offering you 'a safety rope' you can use in any situation, no matter where you are or how bad it looks and feels. Just remember that all states are transient. The more you practice, the easier it will get, and the more Peace you will have access to. With more Peace, you will become more resourceful and therefore more powerful in the face of adversity. This is a certainty.

Can you control your emotions?

No you can't, as emotions are the result of a thought process. You could choose to repress your emotions but we recommend against it, as this is just like a dam, waiting to burst.

However, you can certainly change your thinking, which will naturally allow for better and more Life-enhancing emotions. Overriding one emotion with another is not the best you can do with your wonderful Human attributes, since emotions—if they make you feel less than who you are—are your cue that there are some thought-forms or beliefs in need of being cleared. Remember that your emotions are in fact one of the few direct ways your Subconscious can alert your Conscious that there is a 'bug' in your system. It is a great thing that you can benefit from this timely invitation to let go, as this will be your first signal, which, if ignored, will fully manifest in a physical capacity, so get to see it better. You can compare it to an honest and very well-meaning partner tapping you on the shoulder to get your attention before it is too late.

So instead of pushing down an emotion, or replacing it with the pretence of happiness, be willing to receive its message, and proceed to release it, with gratitude. You could use the following, while addressing your Subconscious: 'Thank you for showing me that there is so much ... in me, I didn't realize that it played such a huge part in my Life. I now release you from it. I love you, thank you.' Please note that the words are not the magic formula here, but your Conscious realization of what is taking place (Step One) and the releasing of the memory (Step Two) is what will set you free.

Thriving, not just surviving

All that you are involved with is really a spiritual game: you, your Life, your work and your business. You get to see different aspects of you and get an opportunity to transform into more than who you are at every occasion.

We wish you to become everything that you came here to be, and our wish for you is that you enjoy the game, the GAME OF LIFE.

CONNECTING the DOTS

PARTING WORDS

MORE THAN JUST A BOOK...

As you may already know, words spoken or written hold a particular frequency, which is significant. The energy behind any words, or any work or person, is even more significant than the words expressed. This book is our energy signature, so you can call it a Key. This means that you can use it in many ways. The obvious first use is to read it, as you have just done and we are grateful to you. We would recommend that, if you are willing to try something different, you might like to 'breathe in' what you read, which will allow your heart to participate in the reading, and not your intellect alone. This will benefit you far more than you can imagine, as it is a very real, practical and a much better way of assimilating information at a cellular level. Information got at a cellular level insures that you allow for core transformation to take place, allowing the breakthroughs you want to experience to have a real chance to manifest in your Life.

As you breathe in information, your two main centers, your brain and heart—both emitting and receiving powerful electromagnetic and electrical energies—can harmonize to allow a powerful shift within you.

Because this book contains the frequency of all that is offered herein, it will harmonize with anything it comes into contact with, so use it as you will, but use it wisely. For example, you can certainly put it with any inanimate thing that belong to you, such as in your car, in your office, in your financial papers, your travel plans, a list of clients, reports of any kind, etc. The only thing we ask is that you do not force it upon another fellow Human Being without their prior knowledge or consent. This means that sneaking it under your husband, wife's, kids or anybody else's mattress is not an option!

Remember that whatever you perceive is yours and yours only, and that you can be more effective for all parties concerned if you will just take care of you. Your whole experience of Life, and the response and attitudes of the people around you, depends on your own perceptions and therefore your response-ability, and not the other way around. In other words, this means that you only need work on yourself, first and foremost, and all else will realign. Things and people can change when YOU change, not the other way around. We hope that this statement is a relief for you as it really puts you in the driver's seat. Each has their own guidance and is connected to Source, whether they recognize it or not, and each seemingly inanimate object is anything but static, as it is also made of atoms and molecules, and is therefore a Life form. The only real control you have is within you. Pressing this book on people may have irritating consequences and cause debates and disputes, minds arguing with minds, armed with beliefs, a war of data! In our humble opinion: a waste of time and precious energy.

Take care of Self first and always. When your 'cup' is filled, you can go out to others and serve. Treat this as you would a journey, and we echo the words you would hear upon embarking on any flight, which is that in times of crisis, put the oxygen mask on yourself first, before attempting to rescue anyone else. This is truer and more multilayered than you could ever imagine.

What about your pets?
Your pets, being an extension of you with a lesser free will, can also benefit from what is in this book, although we would still recommend you ask their permission, however you do that. They are very closely intertwined with you as they breathe in your proximity, and therefore, are an extension

of you, energetically speaking. Arctic the Great, Dugast's beloved dog, certainly enjoys a Life of freedom, no matter if the gate if left open or closed!

This book is not a therapeutic manual,
but a Key to freedom.

Use it as you will.

HEART INTELLIGENCE: THE NEXT FRONTIER

As you may already know, the brain is not the first, but the second antenna that distributes signals to the rest of your physiology. The heart can effectively be considered your first 'brain,' and its magnetic field is thousands of times stronger than that of the brain, and its electrical field hundreds of times stronger than that of the brain.

For the Pioneers among you, who are already familiar with the heart's intelligence, we want to confirm that a 'short-circuited' access from the heart to the rest of your physiology is indeed possible, without going through the filtering of the mind. Although this is rare at this time, it is one of your attributes, and will become more commonly used with the unfolding of your DNA. All of which will be accelerated by practicing the materials included here. We are describing the space of Self-Mastery.

Success is when preparedness meets opportunity, and we know that will enjoy making yourself success-prone!

THE FUTURE OF NOW

Right now you are still living in the Era of Consumerism. Soon enough, however, when all will have witnessed a few more long lasting results ensuing from earlier words and deeds; saving your species from self-extinction will become a very real and global priority. It will bring to the forefront one of the oldest Laws, the Law of Unification, which will mirror externally what is already at work within your own biology, within your cellular network, as discussed in the last chapter. Many countries will learn to cooperate and work together, using communal visions born during think tank sessions to construct a future that is viable for all. Think tanks will have become the most sought after resource that each country possesses. They will be made up of who you would still consider today as 'unlikely candidates' giving a voice to some extremely young, and some very old participants, mixing cutting edge vision with wisdom. You will find that communication will be established between the most unlikely of countries from where you stand today, and cooperation will override division, out of necessity.

It will be not be much longer now before *Connecting the DOTS* and other similar systems will be a staple of early education, giving growing children—citizens—all the tools required to bring about the changes that many of you, adults and elders today, have seeded throughout the years and through much of your suffering. Such teaching will be labelled as 'personal science'—or something similar—and will become common knowledge, as are the basic subjects of today. More students will stay in education and develop their strengths and particular talents at an earlier age. This will reflect into all areas of society, such as politics, health, medicine, agriculture, law, travel, transport, etc., and birth the long awaited New Earth into manifested reality.

ABOUT THE AUTHOR

M. I. Dugast, Ph.D., was born in Chamonix Mont-Blanc, France. She started her life of Service 1994, and has practiced many healing modalities and taught self-development in the past 30 years.

M. I. Dugast is the author of *Mahayana's Rejuvenation Manual*, and *The Rejuvenating Trilogy*. She has shared her work in China, the USA, Hawaii, France, Germany, Ireland, Northern Ireland and the UK. The work shared reflects the fundamental essence of well being, freedom and self-empowerment, and whether it is written or transmitted, anything she imparts is simple, fun and highly practical, so it can be used by anyone wishing to improve their daily experience of life.

CONNECTING THE DOTS FACEBOOK PAGE

Dear Beloved Reader,

You are cordially invited to join us in a special Group on Facebook, especially designed for you as a *Connecting the DOTS* Pioneer! Type '*Connecting the DOTS* – M. I. Dugast' and include the code Pioneer-369 to be invited in, as this is a closed group, reserved to you, the reader. There, you will receive some Inspired tools and remainders not available anywhere else. You will also have an opportunity to dialogue with us and get news of Transmissions, videos and other events at first hand.

We did our best to give you the essence of *Connecting the DOTS*, but much of what we do during the Transmission could not be included in writing as it follows the tradition of oral teachings. So we very much look forward to meeting you, if you do, too, and assisting you on your journey to the expanded version of YOU.

With Love & Peace beyond comprehension.

Mahayana for *Anthenaeis*

OTHER BOOKS BY Mahayana I. DUGAST

Available on Amazon in print and for e-readers

Mahayana's Rejuvenating Manual, *Anti-Aging Secrets*

The Rejuvenating Trilogy Book I, *Acquire the Ideal Weight while you Rejuvenate*

The Rejuvenating Trilogy Book II, *Magical Skin Care & Detoxifying Methods*

The Rejuvenating Trilogy Book III, *Ageless Mind & Conscious Loving*

14700291R00099

Printed in Great Britain
by Amazon.co.uk, Ltd.,
Marston Gate.